JOURNEY TO THE INTERSECTION OF PSYCHOLOGY AND METEOROLOGY

JOURNEY TO THE INTERSECTION OF PSYCHOLOGY AND METEOROLOGY

An Exploration of Weather's Human Impacts

MATTHEW J. BOLTON

Self-published by Matthew J. Bolton

CONTENTS

On the Blending of Weather, Psychology, and Society

Weather used to be communicated simply. Early societies focused on pictorial record-keeping and basic observational forecasting,[1] while oral traditions (folklore, proverbs, and sayings like "red sky in the morning, sailor take warning") and, later, the written word facilitated transmission and characterized understandings of weather information.[2]

Meteorology has since undergone significant change.[[1]] Yet, one need only look to historical disasters like the 1888 "Children's Blizzard" across the middle and upper U.S. Plains[8] (so-named because of the number of children who died as the event unfolded), the Great Galveston Hurricane of 1900,[9] the November 1913 Great Lakes gale,[10] and the 1935 Labor Day hurricane in the Florida Keys[11] to see how information-processing and technology shortfalls in the recent past led to low forecast skill and what we now consider poor meteorological communication strategies.

Even fifty years ago, forecasts were disseminated by tele-type, electronic computers were large in size and slow in speed, and weather satellites had just entered the observational scene. Storm spotting and numerical modeling were in in-fancy, while radar displays lacked the colorization and capa-bilities we know today. Forecasters paid little attention to the impact of their words on end-users. Today, weather profes-sionals emphasize communication skills as fundamental in forecasting, and have an arsenal of powerful tools with which to communicate increasingly nuanced information.

Technology improvements–the introduction of high-cal-iber hardware such as radar, satellite, LiDAR, and atmos-pheric-emitted radiance interferometers, and software–are accompanying rapidly-growing forecaster knowledge- and skill-bases. These advancements all inform decision-making and significantly improve information transmissivity. Factor in the expansion of and increased understanding for commu-nication modes and you have a recipe for the advent of the so-cial science age, at scale, within meteorology.

Meteorologists and social scientists working to improve meteorological communication are rapidly unlocking new learnings about weather's panoply of societal impacts. These include realizations for the varied ways commodities (such as food and electrical power) are affected downstream by, for ex-ample, the amount of water plants need and the effects of tem-perature stress on infrastructure, and for how much weather drives society's outdoor recreational activities. Such focus would have been anathema to forecasters in the early 1900s, when meteorologist Isaac Cline famously neglected to warn Galveston residents of the approaching hurricane.[9]

Even mentioning tornadoes in the forecast was long prohibited by the U.S. Weather Bureau (the precursor to today's National Weather Service; NWS).[7] Thus, "meteorology past" was primarily concerned with physical pattern observation and "meteorology present" now *also* emphasizes understanding of societal processes as part of a constantly-evolving, multi-disciplinary framework for the mass communication of critical and non-critical weather information. Unlike their predecessors, modern weather professionals are regularly exposed to and concerned about the processes of communication–non-verbally, verbally, and in writing–and integrate these into their day-to-day job roles around weather and climate.

New methodologies, knowledge, and concerns all keep discussions of weather and its societal dimensions rapidly-expanding into and across new dimensions. This overall discussion, moving us towards "meteorology future," is strongly informed by concepts and principles from the social and behavioral sciences (SBS; including but not limited to anthropology, the communication and decision sciences, demography, economics, geography, political science, psychology, and sociology) to explain both inner, organizational and outer, public/end-user behavioral responses. It is this collision of concepts I have written about here.

A Few Notes

I wish to clarify a few points which may help readers unfamiliar with SBS concepts. First, psychology is not concerned with *group* differences in the same manner as, say, anthropology, communication, or sociology. It is, rather, concerned more generally with *individual* differences in behavior and the mind which, with repeated observation, are extrapolated outward. Some scholars consider it a distinct scientific field alongside mathematics, physics, chemistry, medicine, and the earth and a set of broader social sciences; others consider it merely another social science.[12] Throughout this book, when referencing non-psychologists, I am typically talking about anthropologists, communication theorists and practitioners, geographers, and sociologists.

Social-behavioral scientists all study people. However, psychology has since its inception possessed a philosophical grounding in the study of inner experiences–thoughts, feelings, and emotions–of individuals and small groups. While there is sometimes complicated overlap–such as social psychology and sociology; industrial-organizational psychology and particular sub-fields of anthropology–the other human-focused sciences tend to be contextually-situated to consider wider society a primary mechanism or cause of the individual's disposition.

Consider the contrasting study of personality by psychologists and sociologists. The psychological view of personality encompasses individual patterns of thinking, feeling, and behaving[13] while the sociological outlook sees personality encompassing the status of the individual within their in-group (the people like the individual, with whom they identify) based on traits and in terms of the individual's self-perceived group role.[14] Put another way, psychological personality considers sets of traits or characteristics that comprise an individual's personhood while sociological personality relates to the way a person's individual traits and attitudes organize to place that person within a group, and to how the person self-represents within the group.

When it comes to the ways the various SBS scientists approach research, there tend to be substantial methodological differences accompanying the ideological-philosophical ones. Non-psychological SBS scientists most often emphasize qualitative or observational data (for example, focus group interviews in which people *describe* their emotions, or observation of a person at work or doing a task) while psychology typically features quantitative data (which can be *measured* with numbers, such as survey instrumentation on mood and well-being) and, importantly, experimental procedures that may include brain imaging, observation, or more prominent behavioral tasks. Weather-focused sociology studies are often focused on subjective experiences, like those of disabled people in hurricane evacuation situations.[15] Weather-focused psychology studies typically seek to measure numerically-quantified relationships like that which exists between personality traits, political orientation, and hurricane evacuation intentionality.[16]

Philosophical and methodological differences aside, I do not believe any single SBS discipline is superior within the weather, water, and climate enterprise–the collective group (which includes meteorologists, emergency managers, social scientists, psychologists, hydrologists, and others) whose individual entities work together to communicate weather information to the general public. Rather, they can co-exist and even collaborate to augment support of meteorologists (to this end, much of my work has been undertaken with meteorologist colleagues). Together, the overlapping fields of anthropology, communication, geography, sociology, psychology, and other social sciences melded with meteorology comprise what is commonly viewed as an integrated weather-social science.

I want to point out that weather-social research exemplifies that science is *never* proven; no single dataset is ever "*good enough*" to explain the mind or behavior, no research question nor hypothesis absolute or beyond inquiry. A plethora of research methods-related issues surround any empirical finding, and there is increasingly an open science movement (see https://osf.io/ezcuj/wiki/home/) seeking to bring transparency to the field of psychology. Psychology is in turn becoming more self-correcting with respect to research practices and the apparent "truthiness" of findings; whole bodies of work and "established" theories, findings, and views are being upended and questioned amidst renewed rigor and attention. By this measure, the science here is open to scrutiny.

I aimed to sort through the weeds and select reliable findings but also include some more preliminary in nature, in the interest of including a larger scope of potentially valuable empirical and theoretical inquiry. I hope you will find this scholarship insightful, but encourage you to remain open about it all and to not attach to any one finding. Rather, consider multiple possibilities as to their true nature.

Where appropriate, I have tried to provide critical analysis
and deeper insight, and highlighted sample sizes to denote
larger and population-representative studies. Publication year
has been appropriately added to further contextualize results,
as well, while references are chronological superscripts and oc-
casionally use a more traditional author/year format. Num-
bered notes are demarcated by superscripted brackets.[like so]
Importantly, note that the presented scholarship is only a thin
slice of the overall psycho-meteorological literature, intended
to give readers a broad look at this area of science. Accordingly, it was inevitable that I could not include every topic area
or every finding with as much detail as some might wish, or
even as I might have wished in some instances. I hope, however, the included material will satiate and even spark readers'
curiosity for this science.

The Psycho-Meteorological Intersection

A 2018 report[17] by the United States National Academies
of Science, Engineering, and Medicine (NASEM), *Integrating Social and Behavioral Sciences Within the Weather Enterprise*, defines the broad social and behavioral sciences as
comprising "beliefs, perceptions, attitudes, emotions, decisions, and actions, as well as interactions with the physical
environment and other people, across diverse social and insti-
tutional contexts" (p. 12). No formal operationalization exists specifically for weather-climate psychology, but since the
work borrows concepts from across psychology I do not think
a higher-resolution formulation is beneficial. Such definitions
help but also immediately constrain areas of study.

I instead highlight work which interests me and which I think is valuable to informing a general understanding of weather-psychology. It is for others to further this thinking beyond what I have envisioned here.

Why This Book?

This book is not the first to cover the psycho-meteorological, or even broad meteorology-SBS, intersection. Still, my approach differs from other authors. Geographer Eve Gruntfest's 2018 textbook *Weather and Society: Toward Integrated Approaches*[18] targets for an academic audience the integration of social science methods into the meteorological domain while, although it includes psychology, the aforementioned NASEM report features a mixed bag of SBS topics and focuses on research-to-operations applications and defining and providing solutions to society-level problems. More relevantly to this book, Trevor Harley's *The Psychology of Weather*[19] and *The Psychology of Climate Change*,[20] by Geoffrey Beattie and Laura McGuire, both published in 2018 in Routledge's highly lay-reader-oriented *Psychology of Everything* series, give very short accounts relating weather and climate to psychology.

Daipha wrote *Masters of Uncertainty: Weather Forecasters and the Quest for Ground Truth* (2015),[21] and Hoffman, LaDue, Mogil, Robber, and Trafton penned *Minding the Weather: How Expert Forecasters Think* (2017),[22] about the psychology and sociology of meteorologists from forecasting and workplace perspectives. Then, there are much headier and esoteric books on climate change, such as Dodds' 2011

Psychoanalysis and Ecology at the Edge of Chaos,[23] Weintrobe's 2012 *Engaging with Climate Change: Psychoanalytic and Interdisciplinary Perspectives*,[24] Orange's 2016 *Climate Crisis, Psychoanalysis, and Radical Ethics*,[25] Hogget's 2019 *Climate Psychology: On Indifference to Disaster*,[26] Zimmerman's 2020 *Trauma and the Discourse of Climate Change*,[27] and Mathers' 2020 *Depth Psychology and Climate Change*.[28]

I have attempted to inform others about these topics in a way that makes sense to me and which strikes a balance between the more academic and lay-titles above. While I have at times blended perspectives, I am focused psychologically and am mostly uninterested in outlining, or providing solutions to, problems. I discuss a few, but prefer instead simply to examine and present for consideration the wide, ever-changing landscape of psycho-meteorological connections.

I aimed in my writing to present a synthesis of research findings for the benefit of student and working meteorologists and emergency managers, and perhaps students of psychology, looking to inform themselves about basic psycho-meteorological connections in a non-technical and timely fashion. I intended, also, to present a book of interest to the general public. Moreover, it is the book I would have wanted when I discovered this research area some five years ago. I hope readers will find it informative and authoritative, with academically-grounded but generally accessible content.

Who am I?

To begin closing this introduction, I want readers to know how my background supports the book's writing. I obtained a Bachelor of Arts degree in psychology from Saint Leo University in 2019 and am currently pursuing a Master's of Science degree there with anticipated graduation in December 2021. Upon graduation, I intend to pursue education qualifying me for licensure as a practicing mental health counselor. One area in which I hope to specialize is natural disaster trauma.

I have had a life-long passion for weather and originally planned to become a meteorologist. While that career did not pan out, I have been extensively exposed to the field of meteorology and involved in the American weather enterprise since embarking my first year of high school on an intensive meteorological self-study (quickly achieving a roughly college sophomore-level education, precluding more advanced atmospheric dynamics and math-theory courses).

Beginning my third year as a high school student, I interned with and then, much later, became the professional collaborator of meteorologist H. Michael "Mike" Mogil, with whom I had a 10-year working partnership at his weather education and consulting company How The Weatherworks. The internship took me to several professional conferences in high school, presenting meteorological research (and I have attended many others since). At the time of my first presentation, aged 17, I was the youngest conference speaker on-record at the annual conference of the National Weather Association (NWA).

I have served in multiple leadership roles at both local and national levels of the weather enterprise: In high school, I was Recording Secretary and chaired the Education and Social Media Committees–and as of this writing am serving as President–of the West Central Florida Chapter of the American Meteorological Society (AMS). I was for several years a student member of the NWA's Professional Development Committee and was a founding member of the NWA Diversity Committee in 2015 (my second term-of-service ends this coming December).

A significant aspect of my earliest weather education included a series of intensive high school summer weather camp programs sponsored by the National Oceanic and Atmospheric Administration (NOAA) and NWS (later, Mogil and I co-directed camps in Southwest Florida from 2013-2020, with the final year being an innovative, first-of-its-kind virtual program during the COVID-19 pandemic).

Other experiential development includes NWS and television station weather center, and county-level government broadcasting, job shadows; weather-related work with an emergency management office; and college-level introductory meteorology courses. My independent study has included Federal Emergency Management Agency (FEMA) courses and certification and numerous professional-level meteorological webinars and associated activities.

My journey in the weather enterprise–a life-chapter which largely closes with the writing of this book, my entry this month into crisis counseling, and Saint Leo graduation, as I transition from academic pursuits and shift my primary focus to the mental health field–has taken me in and out of emergency management centers, television broadcast stations, solar energy farms, NWS offices, and more in exposing to me practically every facet of meteorology.

On a more academic note I've published nearly 40 scholarly papers and participated or been invited to participate in some 80+ conference and other non-conference talks, panels, workshops, school programs, public education events, and online webinars on various meteorological and psychological topics. I have won conference awards for research as well as public speaking. And, I have been heavily involved in nationwide weather learning-facilitation and more general mentoring efforts, especially for middle and high school students. To date, I have mentored over a dozen grade-school students and another near-dozen college students and others in weather, psychology, and daily life.

With all these and other experiences, when I began taking steps towards psychology in 2014 it was only natural I figure out a way to remain close to my original interests. Enter, stage right, my discovery of weather-climate psychology and, now, here we are today. This book's material is informed by empirical research and, to no less important degree, my personal perspective. I hope you will gain a greater knowledge of and appreciation for the work being done at this crossroads, to improve weather communication processes across the vast weather, water, climate enterprise.

With Great Thanks...

The writing of this book was a significant personal achievement–hence the length of this acknowledgment–first undertaken in the last 6 months of my undergraduate studies in late 2018 and completed during the COVID-19 pandemic. The time since has involved traveling a long and winding road to self-publication. The book would not exist were it not for the encouragement and support of Sarah Jane Shangraw–who originally encouraged and prompted its writing–and Mike Mogil, who contributed much to early drafts and formulations. Their contributions and consultations before and during the early writing process were invaluable.

Planning this book while completing the tail-end of my undergraduate studies and then writing over the course of my first year of graduate studies, during a pandemic, was challenging. There were moments in which I felt I was barely treading not-so-shallow waters. I am grateful to my family–parents, Kim and Stacy; sisters, Ashlyn and Emma–words cannot express my gratitude for their support. I am further and similarly indebted to Christel Cruz, Stacie Hanes, Max McClain, and Ellen Ratliff–the steadfast friends whose support and inspiration were invaluable and proof that some chaos is only apparent. I want, also, to thank Patrick Howley and friends in a person-centered encounter group for their profound influence dating back to August of 2020.

I do not have room to thank all of the numerous helpful individuals whose acquaintance I have made on my journey into meteorology and from meteorology into psychology (but, rest assured that if I have met you, you have had impact).

However, I want to thank for countless hours contributed to my life, and innumerable questions answered and concepts conveyed, the most formative mentors without whose influence the book would not be in the form you are reading: Dr. Greg Blumberg, Ken Carey, Nicole Carlisle, Mike Clay, Paul Close, Dr. Jennifer Collins, Barry Damiano, Rick Davis, Robert Garcia, Andy Johnson, Brian LaMarre, Brian McClure, Mike Mogil, Dan Noah, and Dr. Charlie Paxton.

In psychology, I extend gratitude to my undergraduate/graduate research supervisor Dr. Lara Ault, who saw real potential where others saw blind ambition, and graduate co-advisor Dr. Keith Burton; as well as to Drs. Simon Baron-Cohen, Alan Stewart, and Margo Watt; and to my first psychology instructor, Jodi Savell. I am also particularly grateful to a few former students from whom I've simultaneously learned while facilitating their learnings: Dylan Allen, who has demonstrated the benefits of flexible curiosity and the growth that can come from a willingness to learn outside one's comfort zone; Grace, who has taught me quite powerfully about resilience; Jake, who has shown the usefulness of versatility; and, last but not least, my first mentee Nico, whose mentorship first piqued my interest in psychology and who has demonstrated the nature of persistence.

Thank you, all, for joining me on my journey into and through the weather enterprise as both an aspiring student meteorologist and now upcoming, meteorology-adjacent psychological scientist-practitioner. It has been quite the ride and I am sure will continue to be. This book exists because of you and I wish you the best of everything.

* * *

In closing, I am grateful to three anonymous reviewers assigned by the AMS when I previously submitted a version of the manuscript to their book publishing division (amidst concerns generated by the COVID-19 pandemic, I eventually decided to self-publish). I must also acknowledge the support of the NWS and AMS, for their respective sponsorship and awarding of a 2020 graduate fellowship which has supported my tuition and freed me to not only write this book but to pursue other work and opportunities (here, I acknowledge my family's support as well). The views, opinions, recommendations, and conclusions presented here are mine alone and do not necessarily reflect the views of the NWS or AMS. Last, I thank Ellen Ratliff for a discerning structural copy-edit before publication. As for the book's contents, of course, any errors, omissions, or technical inaccuracies are my responsibility.

Fair skies and sunshine to you...

Matt Bolton, May 2021

Weather in Everyday Life

*"Some people are weatherwise, some are other-
wise." Benjamin Franklin (1706-1790)*

What comes to mind when you think about the weather?
Does a mental image of clouds, or rain falling at your house,
form? Do you recall memories of a warm summer day or cold
winter night or imagine the sensation of walking along the
beach with a brisk wind in your face and the sun's rays beating
down?

What about that time you went to the supermarket for
groceries and came out to a raging downpour that left you
drenched and scrambling back to your vehicle? Are you
alarmed–do your thoughts scream back to a time you were
impacted by a tornado, hurricane, flash flood, raging blizzard,
or other extreme weather element?

Have you ever spent time gazing up at the sky, perhaps
as a child lying down in the grass, looking for shapes in the
clouds?[2] Do you fondly reminisce about a childhood spent
jumping through puddles after the afternoon thunderstorms
passed with seeming-clockwork precision?

Everyone thinks about weather–the state of the atmos-phere at any given moment, on a time-scale from seconds to about a month. It is inevitable, for weather affects us all. Impacts influence and affect both the mind and body on small as well as large scales.

At the individual level, people often have their mood influenced by weather and may fear lightning, tornadoes, hail, and the potential destruction wrought by these and other dangerous meteorological phenomena. They may account for the effects of heat and cold through clothing choice or home improvements; ascribe mentalistic states (thoughts, feelings, and intentions, and an overall sense of personhood; for example, "old man winter" and "mother nature") to weather; and seek to enjoy weather's many wonders and forms of beauty. Weather goes on to affect practically every aspect of modern society, including but not limited to city, state, national, and global economies; regional and national infrastructures; transportation; politics; and military decisions and planning.

Perhaps one of the most readily agreed-upon, yet subtle, manifestations of weather's impact, however, has to do with its permeation throughout popular culture. Musicians (ACDC's *Thunderstruck*, Credence Clearwater Revival's *Who'll Stop the Rain*, Led Zeppelin's *When The Levee Breaks*, and Tom Petty's *Louisiana Rain* are just a few that spring to mind) often play on meteorological themes, and meteorologist Nick Walker, formerly of The Weather Channel, has even written original music for the purpose of weather education. "Dark and stormy nights" are a common literary theme, and both painters and photographers have long held weather and nature elements in focus.[3]

Film and television, meanwhile, steal the show. *Mission Impossible 4: Ghost Protocol* showcased a Middle Eastern sandstorm (a habūb, which translates from Arabic to refer to sand that is "blasting/drifting"). Bill Murray plays a broadcast meteorologist in the comedy *Groundhog Day*, and many know the family-friendly *Ice Age* and *Cloudy with a Chance of Meatballs* franchises, and disaster-themed movies like *Twister* (even if some meteorologists and weather enthusiasts have since come to dislike a few of its inaccuracies), *The Day After Tomorrow*, and *The Perfect Storm*. And, who can forget the most famous movie tornado of all, featured in *The Wizard of Oz*?[4]

Weather, further, often helps set cinematic mood. In one episode (S2E17) of *Person of Interest*, a hurricane strands the protagonists (one of whom is posing as a storm chaser rather inadequately equipped with a seismograph... it later serves as an improvised polygraph test) and a disguised serial killer and identity thief in a remote, coastal town. Another (S4E20) sees the protagonist endure nearly fatal hypothermia and hallucinations as a result of extreme cold (and a bullet wound). Recently, the TV show *New Amsterdam* (S1E16) addressed assorted medical emergencies during a major snowstorm.

People think about climate, too, although it has taken on controversy. The prevailing scientific evidence indicates carbon dioxide (CO_2), with a strong human influence, is the primary driver of Earth's recent, pronounced warming.[31-33] The Intergovernmental Panel on Climate Change (IPCC) estimated[33] in 2018 that at then-current growth rates, Earth's average surface temperature would reach a threshold 1.5° C above pre-industrial (1850-1900) averages as soon as within 12 years, by 2030 (but potentially as far out as 2052).

At the time, the IPCC advised with high confidence[5] that "reaching and sustaining net zero global anthropogenic CO_2 emissions and declining net non-CO_2 radiative forcing would halt anthropogenic global warming on multi-decadal times cales[sic]." The IPCC was further highly confident (see insert A3.2 on webpage in note 5) that, should Earth's average temperature exceed this threshold, long-lasting and irreversible damages, including ecosystem loss, could occur.

Yet, even with (and perhaps partially because of) perceptual and external influences upon this evidence, people are often obstructed in understanding the problem of climate change.[34-36] Confusion over fundamental definitions of weather and climate, and terms like "climate change" and "global warming" is common.

Where *weather* references the present state of the atmosphere, *climate* generally references an average of "long-term" and enduring weather conditions of a place (a psychological analogy is that it is akin to one's personality whereas weather relates to one's mood). It is influenced by, and feeds into, regional geography and such things as plant life.

The periods over which meteorologists and climatologists tend to consider these averages are quite substantial, on the order of centuries and many tens of thousands of years (the scale on which ecosystems evolve). One may also think of them as including weather averages over anywhere from a month to a thirty-year period (the NWS and parent agency NOAA, following the World Meteorological Organization, typically consider thirty-year periods in computing climatic "normals"). *Climate change* generally refers to the consistent change in these various long-term averages.

As a result, there are many derivative definitions of "climate" used throughout the scientific world. Some consider only geographic and topographic factors, defining climate in terms of small- and large-scale ecosystems. Others maintain that short-term weather drives meteorological *and* geographical climate, influencing both weather averages and the makeup of places; and also that long-term climatic averages are the basis for what we think of as short-term weather. These competing definitions and frameworks for viewing the changes in weather contribute confusion around climate change and are a barrier to proper understanding of climate-related matters.

Climate, like weather, finds its way into popular culture–especially through literature and in multimedia-based place representations. Consider the palm trees and beaches of Florida, Southern California, and Hawaii (the long list includes *Burn Notice*, *The Glades*, *Magnum P.I.*, and *Hawaii 5-0*, among others) just one example.

Weather and climate prominently feature in video games as well, if not *as* a character then to add character. First-person shooters often use weather to dynamically change the course of play and "fog of war" typically complicates combat in the real-time and turn-based strategy genres. In open-world role-playing/action-adventure games, the plane of play is often so detailed and vast as to have distinct weather patterns and realistically-behaving climate regimes which uniquely affect player performance (in cold regions, player health may be impacted unless wearing the appropriate clothing style, while rain and fog can realistically impede visibility sight lines).

Weather's cultural infiltration is obvious. It is perhaps, then, no surprise members of the general public and other end-users are active consumers of weather information. A 2012 Pew Research Center report[37] revealed that among 16 total news topics, large majorities of Americans, whether or not they closely follow their local news, consider weather the most important news topic.[6] Google search popularity for "weather" as an overall topic mirrors this finding worldwide,[38] being about two times more popular in November 2020 as in November 2004–and this is echoed empirically, as the next two studies show.[7]

A 2009 study[39] by the Australian Bureau of Meteorology found that 53% of a nationally-representative Australian sample (1,761 people) checked the weather forecast daily, and 90% reported doing so at least once per week. In the United Kingdom, 58% (of respondents in a nationally-representative sample of 2,000 people) check the weather conditions or forecast either within an hour of getting up or before leaving their home in the morning.[40] For 7%, it's the very first thing done upon waking up. The average U.K. adult converses about the weather 6 times a week, and women talk more about the weather than any other topic–68% of the time! Meanwhile, 9 out of 10 parents in the U.K. report feeling that their children need to understand how the weather works (but were unsure how to facilitate this themselves).

* * *

People mentally model weather in all sorts of ways. A cognitive model, or to be more technically correct, schema, is simply the internal representation and conceptualization that is formed in the brain by our perceptual faculties in the course of interacting with our surroundings.[41]

People create many different mental models–for themselves (such as the perception you have of yourself as a person), for others (such as your view of your friends or coworkers), for objects, and for events and things that occur in the world. This chapter has highlighted just a few of those that play into people's daily lives with respect to thoughts and feelings, and thoughts and feelings about thoughts and feelings about, weather and climate. As the remainder of the book shows, there are many such schema yet to be revealed.

Theories of Weather-oriented Attention

Ben Franklin was spot on: Some people do indeed pay more attention than others to weather and climate elements. Weather salience, a theoretical concept developed by weather and climate psychologist Alan Stewart, quantifies the degree to which people are psychologically attuned to weather. It is a framework for understanding the attention paid to weather.

Weather salience[42] has 5 primary aspects in Stewart's model: perceptual salience (the degree to which weather is noticeable); valence (concerning a person's emotional response to weather); psycho-emotional attachment (including place attachment and personal significance of individual weather events and meteorological phenomena); and perceptions of both the duration and periodicity of weather elements (that is, how long do they last and to what extent are they predictable?). Curiosities based on needs for information related to, and perceptual experiencing of weather; knowledge; and physical sensitivity and awareness to weather were not originally included in this framework but may also be considered essential components.

Stewart's initial measurements of weather salience add more rigorous support to the public opinion polls conducted in the United Kingdom and Australia. In his two large-sample studies of 946 college students[42] and 1,465 individuals representing the USA,[43] women were more weather salient than men on average. My own research[44,45] suggests that people on the autism spectrum exhibit higher levels of weather salience relative to those not on the spectrum, and that there are some factors–general science interest or psychological disposition for attention-to-detail and patterns,[46] for example–which may contribute to this and also predispose men, at the level of statistical averaging, to experience a greater weather attachment than women in certain settings.

Two examples from Stewart's first weather salience paper[42] showcase ways in which communication processes and weather salience may hold influence based on gender. First, men who correctly distinguished a weather watch from a warning scored significantly higher in weather salience related to information-seeking than did men who did not know the difference; and men who had experienced property damage (and thus were more attendant to their property and the natural environment around them) had a higher sensory and observing attunement to weather than did men without such experience. No such specific, gender-based differences were observed for the women in the study. More generally, and lending credibility to the aforementioned experience-related difference for weather salience and property damage, people who evacuated for a hurricane in the past expressed greater overall weather salience and effects of weather on mood than those who did not evacuate.[42]

Findings reported in Stewart's second weather salience paper[43] suggest people in continental and temperate climate zones are more weather salient than those in dry regimes–which makes sense since these individuals would have more varied weather conditions of which to be aware. The study also showed that weather salience is associated with the frequency with which people seek weather information and forecasts, use forecasts to plan daily activities, seek weather information for varied geographic areas, and use precipitation and temperature forecasts. Weather salience is, furthermore, related to understanding of NWS watch, warning, and advisory (WWA) products.[47]

These assorted findings demonstrate the importance of studying individual differences in weather salience. Such research allows weather messengers to better understand the individual characteristics of different message receivers and this, in turn, enables the crafting of more effective and refined hazard products and models of meteorological communication.

Nature Connectedness

Weather salience is a narrower, more specific manifestation of nature connectedness or relatedness. Nature connectedness represents exactly what it sounds like it should–the degree to which a person feels connected to the terrestrial environment.[48-53] This sense is reflected by a feeling of being in harmony or unity with the natural world and living, nature-based things–with all manner of plants, trees, animals, insects–and by a disposition based on an abiding appreciation for the Earth's natural resources.

A recent population-level study[53] of lifespan-related trends in nature connectedness in the United Kingdom, with 3,919 individuals (including 351 children/teenagers aged 7-15 and 3,568 adults aged 16-95), revealed high nature connectedness from ages 7 to 9 before drops from 10 to 12 and the lowest levels occurring between 13 and 15. Results suggested a duration of about 10 years (ages 26 to 30) for nature connectedness to rebound to age 10-12 levels; then, as suggested by this one study, it evens back out to age 7-9 levels while people are in their 30s (ages 31-40), where it remains high throughout the remainder of the lifespan.

While causality cannot be inferred from these results and this was not a longitudinal study (which would have observed the same individuals over the course of many years rather than sample self-reported tendencies at one time), the authors suggest the influence of normal adolescent development as well as the societal factors of our digital era on their data.[8] This work is supported cross-culturally by findings from three different studies conducted by separate research groups in Canada and China.[54,55] Older adolescents had lower levels of nature connectedness relative to their younger peers[54] and adults had higher levels relative to adolescents.[55]

Higher levels of nature connectedness are associated with a greater self-reporting of psychological well-being in multiple areas. In particular, nature-connected people tend to be subjectively happier[56] and more mindful;[57] score higher on tests of both social and emotional well-being;[48,57] express a more allo-inclusive self-identity;[57,58] and seek greater degrees of personal meaning[59] and personal growth[60] in life. Importantly, these mindfulness, identity, and well-being findings were uncovered while controlling for the potential effects of socially-desirable responding.[9] An allo-inclusive identity is related to hypo-egoic tendencies, which indicate a certain degree of transcendence over a focus on one's Self and a belief in the oneness of all people and things.[61]

A nationally-representative study in England (about 4,000 people) related nature connectedness to psychological well-being as well as to both more general health and greater engagement in pro-environmental behaviors.[62] This aligns with other work in which nature connectedness was associated with health, psychological well-being, and conservation[63] and pro-environmental and ecologically-connective behaviors.[58,64]

Despite these clear associations, still other studies reveal some complicated relationships between nature connectivity, environmental concern, and environmentalism, suggesting situational, childhood-developmental, and contextual factors are at play in determining whether or not one's nature connectedness leads to environmental concern and action. These include whether or not virtual reality-based or other technology has facilitated one's exposure to nature (an image or video of a thing is not equivalent to a full, sense-based experiencing of the thing; see later discussion on phenomenological accounts of weather and climate), whether one has had quality exposure to nature in childhood, and degrees of expressed mindfulness, for example.[48,64-71] In addition, such factors as desire for psychological restoration,[72] cognitive interest in nature,[73] place identity,[74] bio-centric values,[75] and specific beliefs about and experiences in natural environments[76] may also contribute to whether or not nature connectedness results in environmental concern and subsequent action.

Weather-Climate Knowledge and Worldviews

Beyond basic awareness and direct observation of weather lent by sensory perception, knowledge is perhaps the most critical weather salience-related concept because it allows one to form integrated cognitive schemas around weather.[77] Folk science and traditional knowledge and wisdom including mythologies, legends, and folklore, as well as lay-hypotheses—seemingly-intuitive beliefs we come to naturally accept without formal scientific testing—inform weather understanding for both Indigenous and non-Indigenous people.

Samoan islanders have devised a complex seasonal calendar steeped in local mythos and cosmology, and also have systems for weather prediction, cloud-naming (based on physical characteristics, apparent altitude, and shape), and categorization of wind (based on direction and strength).[78] The Mäori tribes of New Zealand have their own extensive glossary for weather conditions,[79] while Indigenous African,[80] Australian,[81] and Canadian[82] peoples, as well as Inuit peoples living in Alaska, have developed meteorological vocabularies and also long relied on oral histories to relay important weather events and climatic history. Other work suggests Malaysian rice farmers have developed skilled sense-based observation and forecasting techniques.[83]

Residents of the United States, meanwhile, are heavily influenced in their day-to-day weather and climate beliefs by worldview and politics,[84] as well as folk science misperceptions and myths (such as the notion that tornadoes cannot traverse large hills and mountains; or that lightning cannot strike the same place more than once).[85-87]

One line of research suggests religious people in the American South tend to have more fatalistic attitudes toward severe weather (and thus lower tendencies for threat response, since events and their outcomes are perceived as uncontrollable).[88],[10] Fatalism, the belief that events are pre-determined beyond one's control, towards disaster exists outside of weather contexts, of course. Most notably of late, we have seen it reflected worldwide in behaviors towards the SARS-COV2/COVID-19 disease.[92],[93] Recent research also shows what is called a Dunning-Kruger Effect on weather knowledge, whereby people, especially those who have lower meteorological knowledge, tend to over-estimate what they actually know about weather.[94]

While there are similarities and differences, cross-cultural and geographical variation in weather and climate knowledge showcases a vast landscape of interpretive beliefs and perceptions which differ based on many factors. We can understand these through social and cognitive psychological, sociological, and anthropological lenses. The processes overlaying beliefs, like communication models–including the one[95] explaining the transmission and receipt of messages by senders and receivers–are important in weather messaging. Equally important, however, are the individual characteristics of the senders and receivers.

I want to begin discussing individual beliefs and perceptions more intensively by briefly sharing a finding from the climate change perceptions arena, which indicates that even while controlling for the statistical effects of demographics and political beliefs, people in areas of warmer-than-average temperature, worldwide, are more likely to believe the average global temperature is increasing.[96] This converges with evidence suggesting that alternating periods of cooling and warming can shift perspectives on whether or not global temperatures are climbing on average (findings indicate this may be associated with political orientation).[97-99]

As in the USA, climate change skepticism abounds in Russia[100,101] and Norway.[102] The same does not hold true in China,[103,104] where a large majority believe the climate is changing for the worse–although there is some evidence for climate-related fatalism there.[103] Climate-oriented fatalism is, indeed, observed in many different countries. It is not just a problem in the United States.[104-106]

Still, even with apparent geographically-localized, perceptual-context, and political effects on perceptions and attitudes, many people around the world consider climate change a serious problem.[107-109] Additionally, the literature shows, that lower-income countries are more vulnerable to climate change-induced weather hazard impacts.[109] Returning to earlier discussion of weather and, especially, climate salience, one finds education (and therefore, knowledge by extension) is the greatest global-scale predictor of climate change awareness.[110]

We can see from even these few findings that there are many potential meteorological influences on behavior. Edwin Grant Dexter (1868-1938) was among the very first to study the varied ways weather can affect people. He investigated relationships between weather conditions and lab-based performance tasks, and between weather and destructive behaviors such as aggression, criminality, and suicide[112,113] Although causality is still unclear (two possibilities being that there are direct physiological effects of temperature on the body, or that there are indirect effects via aggressive individuals having increased likelihood to socialize during bouts of pleasant or warmer weather), the early weather-aggression findings appear at least moderately replicable if not robust.[114-122] Contemporary global data on weather-suicide relationships are mixed, but findings suggest some small effects of temperature on suicidality.[123-126]

Psycho-meteorological research appears to have stagnated after Dexter's passing. It was during this period that the more mainstream psychology research areas saw methodological paradigms related to conditioning and behavioral reinforcers grapple with and give way to cognitivist formulations of language and more mentalistic views of behavior involving inner, subjective experiences.[127] Goodbye Pavlov and Skinner; hello, Miller and Chomsky.

* * *

Weather and Helping Behaviors

A more positive line of work explores the effects of meteorological variables on pro-sociality, with the hypothesis that exposure to sunny and pleasant conditions improves mood through vitamin D intake[128,129] and in turn increases helping behavior.[130,131] Research on this so-called "Sunshine Samaritan Effect" suggests that sunny, pleasant weather conditions foster helping behavior in a variety of contexts.[132,133]

One interesting study supporting this work involves social contagion effects of smiling in pleasant weather, whereby smiling at someone passing in the street appears more likely to elicit a smile in return on days that are sunny than on days that are cloudy.[134]

Effects of Weather and Climate on Mental Health

Historically, research into weather-mood interactions and relationships has been foggy, despite intuitions one might have formed based on some of the aforementioned research and an apparently-strong evidence-base linking pleasant mood to low humidity levels,[135] copious amounts of sunlight,[136-138] and high pressure and temperature readings.[139,140]

Many people would intuitively have weather-mood-health impacts health be "a hill upon which they would die," so to speak, given their own subjective experiences. Much of this research, however, is statistically tenuous. Researchers have largely been unable to establish more than preliminary or speculative statistical relationships between affective (emotional) and atmospheric variables.[139-148] Even within the most well-powered studies–those with participant numbers sufficient to allow reliable detection of, and confident inferences related to, statistical effects–findings for the influence of weather conditions on mood are weak at best and often inconsistent.[147,148]

A nuanced reading of the available evidence points to minor effects of weather on mood and emotionality, including sway on the expression of sentiment in online social media postings. I see this indicating a finding which is not absolute; it only applies for some people some of the time, in certain situations or with particular conditions met. Often, psychologists discount a finding if it does not apply to everybody all of the time. There is a tendency for some in the field to emphasize strict reliability of findings, to expect those that occur to do so with such regularity and precision as to be unfailing–and there is debate as to whether or not weather serves as a reliable mood induction.[147] Reproducibility is a fundamental aspect of any science, but I believe that some findings which present as statistically weaker are wrongly downplayed. This is one.

We have to consider wider context and not simply discount findings, even when their evidence is mixed. Is the mixed evidence proof of the finding's instability or non-existence, or rather the influence of any number of circumstantial differences or confounds in the conduct of the experiment or survey, or something within the participants themselves? Or, is it something else entirely that is causing the inconsistency–something within the variable(s) being studied?

The problems with research into the effects of weather on mood and both mental and physical health lie primarily with variability and the subjectivity of both weather conditions and human experience. Meteorologists and psychologists, respectively, strive to measure these as best they can, but atmospheric as well as human processes are dynamic, chaotic systems which are constantly in flux and evolving.[44,149-152]

The old saying goes that the fluttering of a butterfly's wings in Brazil sets off tornadoes in Texas. That might not be *quite* true–it implies a monumental amount of connectedness which, despite atmospheric "teleconnections," does not exist at the micro-level–but there is still a certain connectivity within both meteorological and human processes. Just look to the human body and psychophysiology for evidence of this.[153]

Individual meteorological and human processes are microscale sub-systems embedded within larger atmospheric and psychophysiological "machines," systems where the individual parts of each contribute to the end-product. The perception of the whole (or gestalt) of the product is dependent on the summed perception of each of the components.

To illustrate the statement's first half, I point to the way that each subsection of the brain networks with other specific subsections to collectively allow and inform our cognitive and perceptual faculties. For example, the primary visual, or striate, cortex in the occipital lobe (on the upper and lower calcarine fissure of the hindbrain) connects to the sensory association cortex where the central sulcus divides the back and front of the cerebral cortex and thus the areas responsible for processing movement, perception, and learning.[153]

Consider, too, how the eye is made up of many individual structures and brain-body interfaces, including the retina–the eye's inner lining, upon which images are focused. The retina and sensory receptors situated upon it stimulate electrical energy being processed as a "picture" of the world by the brain via the optic nerve.[153] Here and elsewhere, each activated neuron fires along an axon and responds to each other related neuronal triggering.

We can look to some simple convective processes within the atmosphere as just one case-in-point illustrating the second half of the statement. Clouds are typically formed when "condensation nuclei," tiny particles consisting of (for example) smoke, salt from ocean spray, pollutant matter, or wind-blown sand or dirt, bond with water vapor molecules riding along a rising "parcel" of air, which can be thought of as being like a bubble.

This parcel of air cools below the dewpoint–also known as the point of saturation–as it rises. Because pressure decreases with height and through the influence of various adiabatic-thermodynamic processes, the air parcel, warm relative to its surrounding environment, expands and loses some of its energy as it gains altitude. The lapse rate, a quantification of the extent to which the parcel cools as elevation increases, then dictates how quickly the parcel cools and reaches saturation (a steeper lapse rate, which can be visualized by imagining a sharply-inclining hill or mountain over the span of several yards, as opposed to a gentler, more gradual terrain shift over a mile, indicates faster cooling and thus a more unstable environment). Once saturation (100% relative humidity) occurs within the parcel, water vapor is able to condense onto the nuclei within and a cloud droplet forms. This process occurring repeatedly at scale results in the formation of what we perceive as "clouds."

I describe a higher level of detail here to showcase the complex steps of just one "basic" atmospheric process. Natural physical laws dictate the thermodynamic, kinematic, radiative, and other processes of the atmosphere so that what we perceive as "weather conditions" appear to us with an image of regularity on short time-scales. In reality, these processes are acted upon by many different forces. For example, as air parcels rise, they not only cool but typically are entrained upon by areas of drier air so that both condensation and evaporation are occurring simultaneously within the parcel. It is when there is more condensation occurring on the nuclei than evaporating from it that clouds are able to form. Cloud formation is, therefore, although governed by lawfulness, an altogether much more random process than is apparent to us on the ground. Sometimes the condensation wins out and sometimes the evaporation wins out.

That cloud formation processes occur over milliseconds, seconds, and minutes–not to mention hours in the case of the strongest thunderstorms–is often lost on us, and this speaks to the second half of the statement above. We may, possessing good visual acuity and with mindful attunement and careful observation, discern the tiny structural changes in a cloud from moment-to-moment.[152,154] Even then, however, when they are salient, and even as we may acknowledge the discrete physical processes playing out above us, these changes are to us on the ground apparently random beyond short timeframes.

We cannot readily and accurately predict the continual formation, evolution, and dissolution of hyper-localized vapor-nuclei clusters as they morph within the cloud in front of us beyond just a few milliseconds to seconds. Sometimes, we may be able to gain glimpses of and sense an apparent predictability within the clouds, but primarily our perception of these movements is that they occur on no obvious timeline. This, to me, is one of the clearest demonstrations of the randomness inherent to weather even as it is in technical respects lawfully dictated.

Awareness and tolerance of this randomness within human perceptual faculties is likely predicated on individualized construals of what *randomness* means conceptually in conjunction with individual weather salience[44,149] and a deeper, more percept- rather than concept-oriented experiencing of *atmosphere*, *weather*, and *climate* as personalized *events*.

Phenomenological accounts of human-nature-weather connectivity,[150-152;154-158] focusing on the personal and subjective perceptions that exist uniquely within each person, understand from biological perspectives[153] that each of us constructs our own filtered reality. Various neural systems within the cerebral cortex assimilate sensations–the raw sense-energies which each living body detects via electrical signals as light, sound, heat, cold, physical touch, and so on–within a unified perception. It is the brain's continual interpretation of this body-based data that we "live" and consider conscious "experiencing."

We thus each personalize the meteorological messages given to us by nature, and, in turn, each perceive the weather and climate in a different way: some people will be more or less cognitively or perceptually attuned; some will be more or less physically sensitive; some will be apathetic and indifferent or overjoyed and ecstatic.[152]

When considering the parallel scientific complexities of meteorology and psychology, as well as unique perceptual experiences of the world, we are bound to find psycho-meteorological phenomena which are intermittently-occurring (just as we do in other areas), such as those dealing with weather, mood, mental and physical health, and emotion. Human variability is simply such that weather will not trigger negative (or positive) effects every single time.[147,148,152]

A layered reading of the weather-mood literature further shows, in addition to the above variability factors, that many different research-associated forces play upon this area of study. At the intersect of emotionality and weather, there are many interlocking parts and contextual features–such as the length of time spent outdoors and the seasonality of the weather phenomena being recalled, thought of, or experienced.

Considering any factor at another's expense naturally alters the study and necessarily excludes some inferential power; we can only ever include so many variables. Moreover, no researcher can foresee every confound or consideration any study might require (which may change as more is learned or other issues or considerations arise). Then, too, survey research on the affective-emotional components of experience is also inherently difficult,[159] as factors within the individual that are unique to emotional self-reporting are exacerbated by other self-report problems including item comprehension, honesty, response accuracy, and impression management.[160]

Beyond more general mood and emotion influences, there is seasonal affective disorder (SAD). SAD is studied by behavioral scientists and medical researchers and involves pronounced season-dependent effects–usually depressive–on one's mood and corresponding behavior.[161,162] Research on global prevalence appears to be limited, but enough data exists that some trends have been identified. In particular–and this makes meteorological sense, given the climate regime transitions occurring as one moves away from the equator–SAD increases at higher latitudes.[163] Interestingly, these differences appear statistically significant (able to be inferred beyond random chance chance) only regionally, in North America, where SAD's prevalence is two times higher than in Europe.[163] European prevalence trends upwards for individuals living at higher versus lower latitudes, but drags the global mean down such that latitude and occurrence are not significantly associated at the global level.

A preponderance of regional evidence from around the world supports this finding,[163-166] as does evidence that major depression, in general, increases with latitude.[167-170] An interesting bio-psychological hypothesis[172] put forth by Alan Stewart, Kathryn Roecklein, Susan Tanner, and Michael Kimlin suggests vitamin D consumption might help to regulate the depressive and seasonality factors involved with SAD. Not only is vitamin D insufficiency associated with depressive symptoms[173,174] but, in a process that is one contributor to SAD at higher latitudes, the body tends to produce lower levels in the fall and winter seasons due to lower levels of UVB-range (290-315nm) solar radiation reaching the Earth.[175-177]

Cognitive-behavioral and light therapies have been found helpful to individuals with SAD.[178-180],[11]

SAD is generally associated with depression, a lack of sleep, and heightened sleep problems such as nightmares.[170] Other research indicates that sustained seasonal variation in mood as can be brought about by SAD might exacerbate chronic medical conditions like diabetes,[171] influence alcohol consumption and abuse,[181,182] and significantly lower quality-of-life for people with physical conditions like low vision and blindness.[183,184]

In fact, due to the reduced light sensitivity of these individuals (caused by interactions between psychological, neurobiological, and genetic factors), SAD may be as much as three times more prevalent among the blind and those with low vision as it is among fully-sighted people.[183] Yet, there is an interesting wrinkle: Blind people, totally lacking in sight, seem to be affected less severely than those who simply have lower vision capabilities.[183,184]

Explanations are tentative within this newer research area, but this curious finding seems to be caused by an innate, neurophysiological photoreceptor cell response, whereby a particular type of cell (intrinsically photosensitive retinal ganglion cells, or ipRGCs) comprising a part of the brain's non-image-forming visual system[12] remains intact for blind people, functioning more fully to take in unconsciously-perceived light than the inhibited conscious sight system of the person with lower vision capabilities.[183,184]

Due in part to these mechanisms, people with lower, but not a total lack of, vision may more easily reach a hypothetical, wintertime-induced threshold for reduced light transduction, beyond which maintenance of their typical mood becomes tenuous. In contrast, profoundly blind people might have their light transduction capabilities so severely reduced that the sight-linked perceptual signal of seasonal mood change is decreased. This, Østergaard Madsen and colleagues hypothesize,[183] leaves blind individuals, somewhat paradoxically to what may be intuitive, less susceptible to seasonal mood shifts that might be induced by SAD.

* * *

In the realm of natural disaster mental health, some individuals have varying degrees of weather anxiety and fear of severe weather phenomena.[186-192] This even, potentially, affects our pets.[193] Strong downslope mountain (such as the chinook and Foehn) and desert (such as the Khamsin in the Middle East and Saharan Africa) winds are believed, meanwhile, to lead some people to express irritation and neuroticism,[194] depression and suicidal ideation,[195] and other, physical effects such as headaches.[196]

Mental health hazards are emerging on the climate front as well. Indeed, although concerns about climate's effects on mental health have existed for many years,[197-209] climate change-related anxiety and grief are two specific psycho-meteorological difficulties associated with existential fears and concerns about the demise of the Earth's natural environment that have only relatively recently drawn scholarly[208-213] and news media attention.[214-218]

Doherty and Clayton suggest[211] climate change-derived anxiety is just one indirect psychological impacts of extreme weather events and persistently-changing weather regimes. Others include worry and depression, despair, apathy, and vicarious (or secondhand) trauma. These exist alongside the myriad meteorological hazards with direct, traumatic effect–hurricanes, tornadoes, winter storms, heat, drought, flooding, lightning strikes, forest fires, mudslides produced by landscape changes, and more. Further outcomes include inabilities to adjust and cope post-disaster; heat-related violence; intergroup conflict; and displacement of individuals.

My own work has begun to focus on ameliorating these harmful impacts of weather-related disaster and trauma, both those that experienced vicariously by weather professionals and the general public.[219-221] In one paper,[220] for example, I, Alan Stewart, and Mike Mogil theorized on emotional processing in the meteorological workplace and the implications of this for secondhand and direct trauma experiences among meteorologists.

A particular emotional processing model considers emotions to be primary, secondary, or instrumental (our work considers the first two). Primary emotions are one's first, visceral affective response in any situation, which may push the person towards outcomes that are either adaptively positive or maladaptively negative. Secondary emotions are reactive responses to the primary emotion. For example, numbness may accompany grief or one may become depressed when angry.

In accordance with this thinking we noted,[220] to show just one example, that weather forecasters might experience grief upon learning of storm-induced fatalities. This would be both "...a positive and adaptive response, because it allows the individual to acknowledge sadness (the secondary response) and move on from an irrevocable loss (of life) outside of the meteorologist's control. However, a maladaptive response might be self-criticism for a missed warning which, rather than triggering desire for learning where one's analyses or assessments went wrong, lends itself to shame and diminished self-worth (the secondary responses)" (Bolton, Stewart, & Mogil, 2020, p. 5).[220]

Another perspective we originated, based in Acceptance and Commitment Therapy and the Individual Psychology viewpoint of Alfred Adler, is that psychological flexibility plays an integral role in meteorologists' on-job trauma-coping strategies. Enhanced psychological flexibility, or balance, is one of the core outcomes desired by ACT treatment. In the ACT perspective, one becomes more flexible through a process of mindfully acknowledging their present experience and, in the face of possible obstacles, committing to meaningful, forward-focused action around their deepest-held values for how they wish to be in the world with respect to that experience. Meanwhile, in Adler's psychology, "the choice of a person to work as a meteorologist reflects the ways that she or he has sought to belong productively with others–to play an occupational role in society and foster what Adler termed social interest" (Bolton, Stewart, & Mogil, 2020, pp. 14-15).[220]

Thus, in response to the news that fatalities had resulted during a severe weather event, an ACT perspective on trauma-coping in the meteorological workplace would posit mindful awareness of the situation, promote willful committing towards one's values, and foster forward-focused action around the goal of the situation based on said values. Adlerian psychologists would suggest the meteorologist's "...healthy, psychologically-flexible choice is to do one's best, acknowledge that action, and move onward (rather than become paralyzed, or freeze)" (Bolton et al., 2020, p. 15).[220] We can separate the Adlerian and ACT-associated flexibilities "...with the analogy to put on one's oxygen mask before helping others. ACT's flexibility would have us help ourselves first [by looking inwards on our experience and reflecting about how we wish to behave going forward, making the choice to act in alignment with our values]; Adler's flexibility would have us help ourselves *by* helping others" (Bolton, Stewart, & Mogil, 2020, p. 15).[220]

Another collaboration with Mogil and Stewart[221] revolved around meteorological education for psychotherapists, to enable a stronger working-with dynamic in therapeutic relationships formed around the psycho-meteorological concerns of the general public and the presentation of vicarious traumatic stress or more generalized life or professional, job-related concerns of meteorologists.

We also provided, based on the humanistic-psychological work of Carl Rogers, a person-centered therapy view of human-weather-climate interactions.[221] Meteorological elements which trouble people "can significantly tear into the substrate, the fabric, that is one's sense of being in the world. Through them, the individual's self-structure [their collective cognitive schemas] and experiences of the world become dis-integrated, leaving the person psychologically unbalanced as well as [potentially] physically displaced" (Bolton, Mogil, & Stewart, 2020, p. 156).[221]

This understanding can be paired with person-centered theory which, in classical terms, sees people become distressed or experience difficulties when their self-structure is out-of-sync or incongruent with their actual experiencing of the world.[221] From here, person-centered therapists can provide a facilitative environment in which the client feels empowered to "formulate for him or herself new internal meanings and schemas for the altering of attitudes, self-concepts, and behaviors" (Bolton, Mogil, & Stewart, 2020, p. 155).[221]

Weather-risk Decision-making

Protective Actions and Weather Warning Response

The needs to make informed decisions in order to react, respond, and adapt to changing conditions, and to appropriately plan one's day, are at the heart of one's weather salience. Yet, the atmosphere is constantly shifting and there is always an inherent degree of uncertainty in all of this responding and planning–who (at least in wetter climate regions) hasn't complained about a sudden rain shower or thunderstorm overhead on a day with a 30% chance of rain?

How do people cope with and adapt and respond to this uncertainty? In an effort to answer this, the section that follows dissects some of the factors affecting weather-messaging uncertainty, emphasizing weather warning response and integrating topics from cognitive psychology and sociology.

Weather warning response is complex and multi-faceted. Most meteorologists and meteorologist-adjacent professionals who deal with WWA products will likely agree that they are often viewed with skepticism (if not confusion) and, at worst, often go unheeded.[222-224,[14]]

Even a brief look at the extensive literature on warning system efficacy and warning response behaviors shows there are many reasons for these tendencies, not the least of which is due to the non-linearity of weather message response. That is to say, although the experience involves common message elements regardless of event type–learning about, confirming, understanding, believing, and personalizing the warning message before responding–individuals do not necessarily follow a set of procedural steps before taking protective actions.[222,224] Once the message is received, warning response components such as those outlined in the following paragraph/list can be interchanged in any order.

One theoretical framework by which to understand warning response is the Protective Action Decision Model (PADM).[225] This theory sees people assimilate various cognitive schemas relating to the warning response process–see bulleted list below–and then further focus these into yet another set of "pre-decisional" perceptions revolving around the individual's exposure to, attention for, and comprehension of the threat:

- Environmental cues (such as the sounds associated with tornadoes)
- Social cues (thoughts which typically motivate action, arising through observation, such as "my friend is sheltering, so I should too")
- Information sources (what is the individual's source[s] for weather information and what are its [their] associated biases?)

- Channel access and preferences for these (by what means–television, radio, smartphone, etc.–is the weather information delivered, and what biases and limitations are associated with these?)
- The hazard warning messages themselves
- Receiver characteristics (the physical attributes, such as strength; visual and hearing, and cognitive capacities and faculties; economic resources, and social supports of the individual receiving the message)

The pre-decision cognitive processes incorporating exposure, attention, and comprehension are in turn focused into yet another set of perceptions about the threat, possible protective actions to be executed, and perceptions of stakeholders (that is, those in wider society with some degree of concern due to the event–such as the government, or the meteorologist[s] or emergency management officials involved in creating and disseminating the hazard message).

These perceptions are thereafter funneled into and comprise the individual's resultant behavioral response to the weather hazard. Finally, once the response has been engaged the individual will (all while being buffeted and impacted by the potential event and situational factors around it) seek out new information, modify the protective response as necessary, and begin to enact coping mechanisms as appropriate and needed in response–not only to the potential event but also any ramifications incurred from preparing for it.[225] Importantly, ambiguity and uncertainty inherent to the message lead people, as they filter it through their own unique set of experiences, knowledgebase, and moment-specific perceptions, to seek additional, confirmatory information.[224-228] It is worth remembering that such models and theories as the PADM are systematic conceptual maps which try to fit complex behaviors into neat boxes and descriptions. Although conceptually helpful, real-world hazard event response is often much messier.

Local television has historically been the go-to, primary source of weather information for most people across different types of hazardous weather event, while emergency sirens also often herald tornadoes.[224] Interpersonal communication traditionally has played a large role across all hazards, and particularly during hurricane[229] and tornado[230,231] events where decisions are quick and technology and electronic messaging often unavailable. Further, as studies in the aftermath of tornado[89,230;231-235] and flood[236] events show, people often feel the need to visually confirm weather-related hazards. Visual confirmation and social network communication often go hand-in-hand; research shows risk perception and response tend to both be enhanced when warning information can be confirmed through different channels.[222,224,225]

Wider situational factors in warning response are important, too. People in the workplace may be most exposed to weather messages through word-of-mouth and interpersonal communication, while college students may be most informed via university email and text messaging (note, this finding is from 2010, before social media became a major conduit for weather information; while university-to-student communications over email remain, social media is often now used to advantage as well).[234]

A further and particularly notorious problem for weather messengers, historically, has been the issue of the night-time tornado (note that the research presented next is only a very small fraction of that which is available on the topic, to which whole books could be dedicated). Although they occur less often than their daytime counterparts, night-time tornadoes are 2.5 times more likely to involve fatalities[237] and more likely, as well, to cause injury.[238]

The vast majority of killer tornadoes, many of which occur in the evening hours (from 1950-2005, 3.9% of nocturnal tornadoes were fatal compared with 2% of daytime tornadoes),[237,239] affect the Southeastern U.S.[85;240-243] There are several key factors that affect protective action capabilities and in turn lead to these fatality rates. Chief among these are that, presuming the warning message is received–barring, for instance, residents being in a deep sleep–both the visual environmental and the social cues which are typically received about and add credibility to the impending threat during the day may be limited.[89,238] Other important issues in this area are both psychological and socioeconomic and affect people whether it is day or night. Low-income, poverty, and poverty stigma–whereby one internalizes negative self-evaluations due to the effects of low-income and poverty–are intertwined and highly problematic psychological and socioeconomic barriers to effective protective action responses regardless of weather event type.

The negative effects of low-income and poverty on weather-related decision-making are well-known: Generally, income disparity tends to be associated with higher fatality rates due to a lack of access to adequate shelter, while other demographic factors (such as language and other cultural barriers; the ethnic makeup of local populations; and the number of people living in mobile/manufactured versus permanent homes in a community) influence disaster risk and vulnerability.[242-247]

While some weather-social researchers have begun investigating links between self-efficacy beliefs (individuals' self-perceptions of their own capabilities) and socioeconomic variables,[243] poverty stigma has not (to my knowledge, at least) been explored in the weather-social literature. However, based on the conjoined effects of poverty lowering self-efficacy beliefs[243,248] and the depression and heightened fear of social support request rejection that poverty stigma can cause,[249,250] we can infer that poverty and its associated stigma exerts a possibly substantial negative influence on protective action responses far beyond one's material resources, by reducing both the extent to which individuals take protective actions themselves and to which they seek protective action support within their social networks. Considered this way, we see both the psychological and sociological in perceptions of weather and an illustration of the complexity of this work.

With respect to tornado warnings more generally, demographic factors and household resources are associated with positive outcomes. In line with the weather salience research and public opinion polls mentioned earlier, Canadian women in one Ontario-based study[251] tended to seek severe weather information more often than men (although most people sampled in the study indicated only using weather products for practical reasons and not paying to weather conditions unless they posed an inconvenience or imminent threat).

Men and women in the United States express roughly comparable levels of receipt, comprehension, and response for tornado-related information,[252] although poor comprehension specifically pertaining to warning areas (which are defined on U.S. weather maps–typically region-based, county-level displays and radar screens–by polygon-based shapes) sometimes causes confusion.[253]

Interestingly, a contradictory finding,[251] possibly linked to cognitive factors mentioned earlier (heightened attention to and understanding of technical aspects of forecast information),[44,45] is that men appear to place more confidence in their comprehension of hazardous weather information. In terms of demographics, people aged 50 and older are more likely to receive warnings via television[254] and to trust the NWS as a source of information,[255] whereas younger individuals–who have greater cell phone access and technological knowledge–appear to prefer mobile devices for the receipt of weather messages.[251,254,256-259] Indeed, smartphones are an increasingly important weather messaging tool.

For tornado-related perceptions more generally, I recommend a series of comprehensive studies on U.S. residents' tornado warning reception, comprehension, and response tendencies by Joe Ripberger and colleagues.[260-263] For further discussion concerning generalized protective action behaviors, I point readers to reviews by Sherman-Morris (2013),[224] Lindell and Perry (2012),[225] and Brotzge and Donner (2013).[226]

Uncertainty in Forecast Messaging

Weather information is typically communicated through numerical and categorical expressions of risk (that is, "X percent chance for threat" versus, for example, X threat is likely/unlikely"). Although academic researchers, meteorologists, and communication practitioners and theorists have long debated which method is most appropriate, it is prudent to say both modes of communication are utilized depending on the specific message and event.[264] Probability of precipitation, for example, as well as many severe weather threat indicators, can be expressed both ways.

Evidence for the use of numeric expressions of risk exclusively over those based in language is relatively mixed and, in any case, a range of communication strategies exists in the real world. Anecdotal discussion and observation in the field reveals some meteorologists prefer numerical forecast information while others, typically TV broadcasters, have stopped using numbers altogether.

The research literature shows that end-user message trust and decision quality generally improve with the inclusion of numeric probabilities in forecast messages.[265-268] However, though the ways in which it is interpreted vary,[268-275] descriptive, categorical language is often better understood by non-expert lay-users.[276-278] There is some evidence that a multi-pronged approach incorporating both approaches is optimal, to offset issues incurred by either alone.[275,276]

Beyond what is reflected within the above data, one psychological basis for the use of multiple messaging strategies is lack of numeracy, or mathematical-statistical literacy.[279] Without even accounting for the prevalence of mathematical disabilities (i.e., dyscalculia), occurring in some 3-6% of the population,[280,281] the USA has one of the world's lowest numeracy rates. A 2013 special report commissioned by the U.S. Department of Education revealed numeracy performance well below the average of, and higher than only two other, surveyed countries in a comprehensive, 24-country international survey.[282,283] The report estimated poor statistical understanding is a problem for over a third of Americans. Conversely, about 4 in 5 United Kingdom adults report low numeracy levels.[284,285]

Numeracy, essential for the interpretation of probabilistic forecast information, is associated with risk comprehension.[264,286] A recent study on the relationships between numeracy and individual differences in numeracy, general educational attainment, and cognitive ability indicates, preliminarily (the authors are cautious in making their theoretical inferences, citing concerns with statistical power), that while people tend to comprehend numerical forecast information without too much difficulty even with lower levels of general education and cognitive ability, those lower in numeracy *do* have trouble interpreting numerically-based forecast information.[264]

An aid to the comprehension of numeric data among non-expert lay-users may be the inclusion of "predictive interval" forecast data.[286] Predictive interval forecasts show the upper and lower bounds within which the observation is expected to occur. For example, one might see a forecast high temperature of 71°F that has an interval high/low error range of 68-73°F. In three studies, Savelli and Joslyn showed that the use of predictive intervals in text-, but not visualization-based forecasts, enabled better identification of unreliable forecasts and that participants using intervals were more decisive in making temperature estimations than those using single-point forecast data.

Weather Warning Compliance

Uncertainty plays a critical role in weather warning response compliance as well as in the comprehension of warnings. A study by Nagele and Trainor,[253] examining warning compliance in a sample of individuals affected by tornadoes from 2009 to 2011, found that the likelihood of seeking shelter was no greater for those within the warned area than for those outside of it but within the county affected by the tornado. Only about 40% took shelter. It was noted that the proximity of the tornado's track to individuals was a contributor to this behavior, as people judged whether or not to take action based on the closeness of the threat–being within 5 miles of the tornado had a significant effect on increases to protective action behaviors.

Furthermore, smaller warning polygons were associated with increased protective action, including sheltering behaviors. This would seem to suggest people perceive such immediate "nowcasts," or forecasts for a time period out to 6 hours from the time of issuance, as more specific, confident, and certain to occur. Together, these findings imply that threat proximity and perceptions of certainty interact to allow a greater personalization of the threat, or perhaps allow better confirmation.[253]

Another example, from the hurricane response literature, involves interviews with survivors of category 4 hurricanes Andrew and Hugo.[287] Only 42% of 777 adults evacuated their homes. Meanwhile, a 2013 report by the City of New York revealed that only 33% of interviewees living within the lowest-lying evacuation zone in the city left as Hurricane Sandy approached in 2012.[288]

Similar research findings have been uncovered with respect to flood warning response,[289-292] while Joslyn and LeClerc (2013) discuss hurricane evacuation non-compliance as involving a combination of factors including, but not limited to, a tendency for risk-seeking in situations involving various types of cost (not just money, but time, energy, and other material resources).[267] Hurricane evacuations in particular can be expensive, involving extensive investments of energy, travel costs, highway dangers, property loss, lootings, and other inconveniences and uncertainties.[293,294]

The combination of these costs and difficulties with the pressures of decision-making under uncertainty, for a choice that is typically made well in advance of the potential hurricane event, tend to push experts and lay-users alike to assume irrational levels of risk.[264,295-297] Compliance can also be significantly influenced by context (especially end-user message trust and knowledge factors),[253,298] as well as by situational forces: One cost of hurricane evacuation is the possibility of losing one's pet. People often take animal ownership into account when deciding whether to evacuate, and while there are those who will decide against evacuating because it would mean leaving a pet behind, many evacuees take their pets with them and tend to go shorter distances than those evacuating without animals in tow.[299]

Disabled individuals often face extreme hardship that prevent evacuation compliance. In 2002, van Willigen and colleagues compared[300] the hurricane evacuation experiences of North Carolina residents who had a disabled family member living with them to residents who did not during Hurricanes Bonnie, Dennis, and Floyd. Reported evacuation rates ranged from 9-25% lower for households with a disabled family member. Contributing factors in the non-evacuation decisions included transportation issues and a dearth of accessible shelters. This aligns with findings[301,302] that disabled individuals are less likely to possess evacuation plans, seeming to hint at wider problems relating to social support for, and/or in the design of educational and outreach materials on, evacuation procedures. Indeed, the needs of disabled people are often met poorly by preparedness and post-disaster response officials.[15,303-306]

A more general problem brought to compliance by uncertainty, related to message trust, is the so-called "cry wolf" effect whereby individuals hesitate or fail to respond to warnings due to previous experience with false alarms.[298,307] A weather-related false alarm is any event which is forecast to occur but does not.[308,309] These come with their own communication difficulties, as illustrated by the finding that many people incorrectly believe the term "false alarm" means there never actually was a threat (rather, the event not occurring *does not* mean it could not have).[310]

In response, a number of research endeavors have been undertaken, including work with people in the same county as, but outside the specific warning area of, specific tornado warnings. This research finds that people outside of, but near, warning polygons often think they are actually within the warned area.[310] The weather-warning cry wolf effect and its relation to false alarms, however, is beyond this book's scope to review in great detail. For detailed learning, interested readers will benefit from work by Simmons and Sutter (2009),[238] Barnes, Gruntfest, Hayden, Schultz, and Benight (2007),[306] Brooks and Correia, Jr. (2018),[307] and Brotzge, Erickson, and Brooks (2011).[308]

Finally, a recent (2020) German pre-post test-based study[15] with 614 participants revealed some complex results with respect to the receipt of warning messages.[311] Perceptions of risk (perceived severity, anticipatory worry about events, emotions anticipated to be felt during events, and perceived likelihood of events) were measured across 5 different hazard types (severe weather, which is of course the focus of this discussion; acts of violence; breakdown of emergency number; discovery of a World War II-era bomb; or major fire). Severe weather was reported as the most likely of the events to occur, and participants indicated they expected these threats would be associated with the lowest levels of negative emotionality.

Overall, receiving a warning message (regardless of event type) lowered anticipated negative emotionality for the period *of the event* but increased antecedent anticipatory worry and perceptions of perceived event likelihood.[311] This suggests people predict they will respond less negatively *during* than before the event, that they will be calmer when the event is unfolding than before it occurs. One interpretation is that when they are experiencing the event itself, people's previously uncertain perceptions of threat are confirmed, denied, or in other ways solidified and they adjust their response accordingly.

In addition, people will have had time, hopefully, to prepare, since that and the provision of a sense of safety via protective action recommendations and advice for appropriate courses of action is the purpose of warning messages. The increasing perception of event likelihood upon receiving the warning message makes sense since the warning message serves to let people know what is on the way; of course once they have been told, they will be more likely to believe it will happen. Of further psychological importance and worth noting for the context of weather messaging, there was an interaction between trait, or dispositional, anxiety and perceived event severity: For participants lower (but not higher) in trait anxiety, receiving warning messages was associated with a decrease in perceived event severity, suggesting perhaps that the message containing particular details of the threat helped ease event-time worries by lending certainty. Those high in trait anxiety appeared to remain vigilant to severity even after learning about the expected impacts, regardless of the event to which they were exposed.[311]

To close this section, a few other relevant research findings include that perceptions of event severity influence decision-making judgements;[312] that compliance with tornado warnings is associated with the number of warning sources one has, whether or not one is at home during the tornado, one's past experiences with tornadoes, and gender;[313] and that heavy cognitive load while carrying out multiple tasks appears to hinder weather warning compliance.[314]

Put another way, this compliance and any associated protective actions and, therefore, warning effectiveness, are hindered when one does not have the mental capacity to take action due to preoccupation with other concurrent actions, thoughts, or feelings.

Another type of cognitive load–actually, cognitive *distraction*–is associated with reduced workplace productivity. A series of studies from 2014 suggest that when inclement weather, such as a typical rain shower or thunderstorm, strikes, individuals are more likely to focus on their work and be productive. Four datasets–from fieldwork at a bank in Japan, 2 online labor market surveys in the U.S., and a U.S.-based lab experiment–support the hypothesis that gloomy weather conditions reduce daydreaming about engagement in outdoor activities and in turn increase productivity (anecdotally, some of us may have experienced this working from home over the last year of the COVID-19 pandemic; I know I have).[315]

Framing and Adapting
to Weather

Increasingly important, expanding, and overlapping with both warning response and uncertainty, research into the framing of weather messages (that is, how they are contextualized, targeted, and communicated to different audiences in various situations) is of much interest. In psychological terms, frames are linguistic devices designed to dictate what is salient to us and thus what influences our judgement.[316-318]

Essentially, frames activate cognitive associations between terms and concepts. A brief demonstration comes from Schuldt and Roh.[319] With respect to climate change perceptions, they found that U.S. conservatives tend to associate heat-impact concepts and imagery (such as rising temperatures and visuals of melting polar ice) more strongly with *global warming* than *climate change*. Liberals tended to associate these impacts equally for both phrases. Framing research spans several disciplines such as psychology, economics, and business so I have tried to focus this discussion.

The emerging research on weather message-related framing actually presents some paradoxical findings. A 2018 study by Joy Losee and Susan Joslyn, for example, investigated the ways that features of weather forecasts influence trust in forecasts.[320] They found that increased severity of the forecasted weather, consistency of the forecast, and decreased familiarity with the forecasted type of weather are associated with increased trust in the forecast. Moreover, greater weather condition severity, perceived inconsistencies in the forecast, and greater degrees of trust in the forecast led to higher likelihoods of protective action among study participants.

So far, so good. When the message is consistent, weather conditions are more severe, or people are not familiar with the imminent threat, they place more trust in the forecast; and when the forecast somehow does not make sense, the conditions are more severe, and the forecast is trusted, people take action to protect themselves. A series of three studies, reported by Burgeno and Joslyn (2020),[321] however, while continuing to suggest consistency evokes trust, also showed that inaccuracies brought about by efforts to ensure consistency actually reduced trust in the forecast.[16]

Participants showed a lack of trust for the forecasts that were inconsistent, but showed an even greater lack of trust when forecasts were perceived as inaccurate. Burgeno and Joslyn concluded forecasters should not favor consistency at the expense of accuracy. These findings, altogether, underscore the complexity of framing effects on end-user forecast trust. Even so, complex results can be helpful in explaining other findings which may elude initial interpretation.

Dylan Allen, as part of a two-year internship experience he undertook while I was at How The Weatherworks, conducted for his "capstone" project a small study into hurricane evacuation behaviors.[322] Interested in answering questions about media effects on evacuation decisions, we tested whether or not intuition, which involves faster and more emotional thinking, interacted with emotional hurricane news reporting "in the field." We predicted that people higher in intuition would be more likely to evacuate when presented with more emotional field reporting. Instead, generally-emotional field reporting led to greater evacuation likelihood. Then, intuition was significantly and positively correlated[17] with media trust, home attachment, and weather fear—and media trust and both weather and hurricane fear were also significantly and positively correlated.

Our data did not allow strong conclusions about the relationship between media trust and the two fear variables. Unknowingly aligned with Losee and Joslyn's research, of which we were then unaware, and with that of Burgeno and Joslyn, which we did reference, we surmised that our participants increasingly saw the meteorologist as an authority figure and that perceptions of message inconsistency, storm severity, and trust played into our results.[322] Our results also hinted at differences in risk perception for coastal versus more inland residents, as highlighted more recently by Emily Mongold and colleagues,[323] and may also be related to differences brought about by media-psychological risk perception effects linked to broadcast meteorologists specifically.[324]

Forecast and weather hazard message features and contexts affect the ways in which people communicate weather messages past their points of origin and determine how far and wide they spread. Traditionally, as has been mentioned, both critical and non-critical forecasts were spread through television, print newspaper, radio, and word-of-mouth. More recently, as smartphone use and wireless capabilities have grown, the Internet and social media have largely wrested popularity from print news and radio as sources of weather information.[42,43,257-259,325]

Weather message consumers are increasingly on-the-go and desire quick and easy access to hazard and threat alerts which are straightforward to understand. Answering this call, wireless emergency alerts (WEA)–short, to-the-point text messages about some imminent threat, often weather-related but also concerning child abductions and other location- and time-sensitive emergency events–entered the scene in 2011.

A host of matters–benefits, problems, proposed and potential solutions to those problems, and much discussion–have arisen around these alerts, and the emerging scholarship involves communication theory, behavioral and psychological responses, linguistics, and more. Rather than attempt to slice and dice a winding and meandering path through a swath of discussion pieces, I recommend a number of highly informative guides, publications, and working papers pertaining to WEA messaging for further learning.[326-331]

* * *

Weather on Social Media

The transmission of weather information on social media has, as with framing, become a substantial subtopic of weather-social science in recent years. Researchers have especially focused on uncovering factors that influence weather forecast and meteorological hazard message transmission among social media users.

One 2019 study by communications scholar Jeannette Sutton and colleagues[332] found that Twitter users most often share, or "retweet," actionable message content, information about historical weather facts, visual imagery (such as a map or infographic), and information which includes named event tags (such as #HurricaneIrma; most social media platforms have adopted some form of such "hashtags" [as we now commonly refer to as pound signs] to enable searching of public posts). In contrast, messages including more general forecast and nowcast content and messages that are sent in reply to other users are shared at a lower rate. Sutton and colleagues have also been active on the WEA front.[333-335] Other scholarship looks at the evolving conceptualizations and coverages of risk by the mass and social medias,[336] the role of visual risk communication factors such as attention and message comprehension in tornado decision-making,[337] and the utilization of social media by the NWS.[338,339]

With respect to social media messaging and communicative framing, the nature of the Internet has given way to so-called "social-mediarologists." These individuals are typically, but not always, amateur weather enthusiasts who run weather-oriented Facebook and Twitter accounts.[340-342]

While many are aspiring pre-college and college-level student meteorologists; sometimes non-degreed-or-certified, but weather-passionate storm chasers; or more general weather enthusiasts who mean well and take care to distribute reliable information; others irresponsibly post extended-period numerical weather model graphics, frequently proclaim imminent weather and climate disaster, and/or post overly-edited severe weather photos or video.

Others incite arguments, or give "takes" they know will be controversial. Many are drawn to the celebrity of meteorology–to the notion of being the "face" of their local weather–including some who merely seek "likes," reactions, and internet virality and notoriety. Within this "mediarology" are characters who far better fit an "internet troll" moniker–among these both climate skeptics and alarmists who, regardless of their perspective, share posts, stories, and videos that may or may not be truthful.

These and other factors–such as information not being adequately sourced and attributed in these social types of re-messaging–contribute to the widespread online proliferation of weather-climate misinformation (psychologists Gordon Pennycook and Sander van der Linden have relevant bodies of work on misinformation, some of it related to climate change, which may interest readers).

It is not all nefariousness, however, engineering social media confusion. An equally if not more troublesome problem–which cannot necessarily be counter-messaged or effectively filtered against–is the nature of social media algorithms that prioritize the display of content based on various popularity- and interaction-centric metrics and actions.

Increasingly, Facebook limits page post reach unless the owner pays a fee to "boost" individual posts. Because of these mechanisms, one often sees content from days earlier displayed atop one's content feed, superseding or interspersed with newer content. Such algorithm-based display tendencies are highly problematic where critical weather watches and warnings, and more general forecast information posts, are concerned; they undermine social media as an effective tool in weather messaging.

Weather messengers will increasingly contend with algorithms designed to prioritize content in certain ways detrimental to hazard messaging. And this doesn't even take into account the overwhelming firehose, the sheer volume, of weather information that is available and which one must sort through as messages are transmitted and re-transmitted and transmitted and re-transmitted and transmitted and re-transmitted and transmitted and re-transmitted and transmitted and re-transmitted... Any attempt to gather weather information from social media means becoming awash in a veritable flood of conflicting and duplicated data streams. Even those who are meteorologically "in the know" sometimes have difficulty navigating the deluge.

Closing Remarks on Decision-Making, Uncertainty, and Framing

Bringing attention to bear for one more discussion in the areas of uncertainty, framing, and weather risk-messaging, there is evidence to suggest that the affect and availability heuristics interact to impact the ways in which meteorological hazards are perceived.[311,343] Heuristics are simple rules by which people make quick decisions, and these two are based in emotion and memory recall, respectively.

For example, in the German risk perception study above, the authors surmised an effect of the affect heuristic in interpreting some of their pre-test results with respect to ratings of emotionality and perceived severity. They suggested that, rather than being associated with the study's contextual frame, these were induced by participants' primary reliance on personal experiences or prior knowledge.

When engaged, meanwhile, with the availability heuristic, which operates based on immediate recall of past events, people are influenced in their present-moment decisions by their present-moment recollection of past events. One consequence of this is that individuals who have not had relevant past experiences make biased and lower quality decisions.[344-347] This is just one reason why people respond poorly to climate change extremes; although individual weather events are not new, the concept of climate change is a newly dawning, existential threat with which people cannot contend based on recall.[348]

Cognitive biases stand alone, but these two can also merge to create a more powerful effect. In contrast to either effect on its own, a combined affect-availability interaction sees past events remembered in a more vivid, more emotionally-powerful and laden manner due to perceptual extremity of the event.[343,347] Individuals thus impacted seem to judge risks more intensely.[343]

To close this section, a few newer and exciting study areas with respect to framing and meteorological communication revolve around the use of rhetoric, language, design elements, and end-user perceptions of and knowledge about visual forecast communication processes[348-354] and by broadcast meteorologists on television.[355] Other work considers the role of politics in shaping and fomenting suspicion around the need to evacuate approaching hurricanes,[356] examines the part played by social networks in hurricane evacuation message spread[357] and how people perceive weather radar;[358,359] and weather professionals continually work to expand views on what it means to craft a consistent message.[360]

My own work with meteorologist Stacie Hanes has considered best-practice methods to deliver effective weather education to individuals on the autism spectrum,[361] and she, Mike Mogil, Grant Wise, and Greg Blumberg have at times joined me to examine message consistency impacts, concerns, and implications for those with color vision processing differences (that is, color blindness).[362,363] Relatedly, others are beginning to more thoroughly consider the weather-related needs of blind as well as Deaf and hard-of-hearing individuals,[364,365] and the NWS is extensively working within Deaf and hard-of-hearing-communities to further weather messaging comprehension in those populations (see https://www.weather.gov/wrn/dhh-safety).

* * *

Adaptation of Behavior Based on Weather Conditions

One line of interesting work I want to briefly showcase deals with people's behavioral adaptations to changing weather and climate conditions. Perhaps the most remarkable of the work surveyed is a 2013 Belgian study.[366] Cools and Creemers suggest people are less likely to change their travel-related behaviors based on forecasts acquired ahead of time than they are to adjust in-the-moment based on observed, current weather conditions (regardless of forecast source and perceived forecast reliability).

To highlight a few points, specific behavioral adaptations depended on the type of trip: Work, school, and leisure-based travel was liable to be postponed; shopping tended to be canceled. No statistically-significant effect of weather type (below-freezing cold; snow; rain; fog; warm temperatures above 82°F; severe thunderstorms) was observed on behavioral adaptation for work or school travel; shopping was significantly affected by rain, snow, and fog; warmth significantly increased leisure.[356] Participants made the most travel mode changes (for example, from public transport to personal vehicle) for snow and warmth; and shoppers adjusted trip timing based on rain and thunderstorms, and adjusted their shopping location based on foggy conditions.

This work suggests, where weather-travel impacts are concerned, that people appear to consider sunk costs–that is, whether they had already invested time or money into the outing–alongside their mobility and personal senses of agency: Owning seasonal tickets/passes for public transport decreased route changes, whereas having a driver's license increased a person's chances of changing shopping transport mode (from public to personal vehicles) and making leisure route changes; license ownership also decreased shopping trip cancelations.[366] A 2017 study found Georgia and Virginia residents using NWS wind-related WWA products were more likely to alter their plans for high wind watches as opposed to high wind advisories (this finding is fading as the NWS revamps the WWA system, but I mention it for the historical record).[47,[14]]

Pondering the Belgian results in particular, it is easier to understand, or at least more readily imagine, how weather might affect blind individuals, and those with lower vision capabilities, in their day-to-day life: Since they cannot access the same resources as others, these individuals will experience greater disruption to their schedules and need higher degrees of flexibility and planning to compensate for last-minute changes caused by inclement weather.

Other research considers the effects of adverse weather on roadway-driving behavior,[367-369] bicycling,[370,371] and vacation-taking and tourism.[372-376] Some research has even investigated the psychology of recreational storm-chasing (within the context of tour-based companies).[377-380] Storm-chasing tourists are driven by a passion for severe weather; the desire to witness spectacular sights, have exhilarating encounters with nature, and witness once-in-a-lifetime phenomena; the challenge of intercepting such difficult-to-forecast meteorological phenomena as tornadoes can be; and to be reminded of humanity's utter powerlessness over nature.[379]

Recreational storm chasers are also motivated, in descending order from most-least, by (1) enjoyment of nature; (2), learning about storms; (3), thrill-seeking; (4), the ability to be with like-minded people (perhaps fulfilling a need to belong); (5), risk-taking; and (6), a sense of achievement (that is, challenging oneself, improving one's confidence, and to both prove to others it can be done and do something impressive).[380]

Weather and Political Voting

A common lay hypothesis that has surprisingly been the subject of little study, but which has become engrained over the past several decades thanks in part to weather historian David Ludlum,[381],[18] is the effect of weather on voter turnout. Ludlum observed, for example, that weather had a crucial influence in the 1960 election pitting Kennedy against Nixon: With a cold front draped across the Midwest bringing heavy rains to key swing states, Kennedy narrowly defeated Nixon as rural Republican voters opted not to go out in the elements (whereas urban voters–mostly Democrats–did). A number of similar observations led Ludlum[381] (p. 102) to remark that "...a rainy day favors a Democratic candidate since the upstate Republicans would not turn out in full in inclement weather, while the urban Democrats would not be put to undue inconvenience."

* * *

Has this observation stood the test of time (and voters and the weather)? The most comprehensive U.S.-based test of this hypothesis, by Gomez, Hansford, and Krause, suggests[383] that rainfall significantly reduces American voter turnout by just under 1% per inch received above the Election Day climatological average while turnout is decreased by half a percent per inch of snowfall above the average. Their analysis further suggested, counter to Ludlum's belief, that rainy weather actually benefits Republican voters; however, more recent work (by Bassi, 2013) puts this conclusion on shaky ground.[384]

A smaller, Kentucky-centric study[385] also affirmed meteorological effects on voter turnout, although work by Fraga and Hersh contradicts it and suggests these effects may not hold for particularly competitive elections.[386,[19]] Considering the overall mixed evidence for meteorological influences on voting behaviors this, in my view, is another effect that might affect some people some of the time (especially considering the political climate of late). Many variables are influential here (including individual sense of civic duty, not measured in any of these studies). It is easy to see how some, but not all, people may be deterred by inclement weather in the course of voting.

In the limited body of international studies addressing this question, the same 1-inch-over-average/~1% detrimental effect on voter turnout is present in the Netherlands,[389] although the Dutch also see an almost 1% *increase* in turnout for every 10°C gained and a 1.5% turnout increase in completely sunny, pleasant conditions.[20] Another study observed no effect of rainy weather on Swedish voters.[391]

* * *

Some research[384] takes a decision-making approach to questions of weather and voting, looking not at voter turnout but, instead, at voting habits as influenced by weather-induced Election Day mood. After controlling for policy preferences, partisanship, and socioeconomic factors, results from Bassi's 2013 study suggest that inclement Election Day weather decreases tolerance for risk, which in turn increases risk aversion and the likelihood of the voter endorsing the candidate deemed to take fewer political risks.

The inverse was true for good weather conditions: For those participants assigned to the good weather portion of the study, risk-taking in the experiment increased, and so did votes for the candidate deemed to take more risks. Results further suggest that when voters might consider switching from riskier to safer candidates, inclement weather could foreshadow a twice-as-large probability of choosing the safer candidate.[384]

Weather and the Stock Market

The above finding that pleasant weather foretells risk-taking could hypothetically be linked back to the earlier research on weather and criminality; and so, too, could it be linked to the stock market. A 2003 study[392] by Hirshleifer and Shumway refueled the weather-stocks research intersection underway since the early 1990s,[393,394] revealing a strong association between sunshine (but not rainfall or snow) and stock returns for markets in 26 countries over the period from 1982-1997, such that investors traded more aggressively on sunny days.

A newer, more comprehensive and sophisticated analysis[395] from September 2019 shows, however, no effect of seven weather variables on eight currency pairs and five market indices, with the authors suggesting evaporation of past observed effects as investors tried to manipulate them for gains (in much the same way past psychological findings may have dissipated in the face of recent cultural and societal shifts).

* * *

Investing isn't the only consumer-related area at the mercy of a rainy day. These relationships are older and thus no longer as relevant with the advent of online shopping, but research from 2010 suggests sunlight also appears to influence mood by inducing positive affect and, in turn, consumer shopping expenditures.[396] Even older Australian research (2001) shows shopping behaviors are affected by rainfall and temperature.[397] Considering how much more widespread the use of services like those provided by Amazon and similar companies is today, it is worth noting that online shoppers can be affected indirectly by weather when inclement conditions delay and even prevent package delivery via road, rail, and air.

Physical and Health Impacts of Weather

Close to but not quite related to weather-climate effects on mood, weather very often has a short-term physical impact. Especially popular in Europe, the term "meteoropathy" has been used to describe these effects[398-401] relating to physical pain and a range of neurological and neurobiological conditions (such as anxiety, stress, depression, headache, and heart conditions; and negative outcomes including suicide).

Mazza and colleagues[401] stated in 2012 (p. 103) that the term "is used to indicate every pathological dimension in some way related to weather conditions," and that meteoropathy "can be considered a syndrome... represented by a group of symptoms and pathological reactions that manifest when there is a gradual or sudden change in one or more meteorological factors in a given area." They remarked[401] on meteoropathy's typically 1-2 day course and apparent higher prevalence among women,[402] onset heralded by sudden weather change, and describe symptoms including increased depressive tendencies alongside potential "weakness, hypertension... increased susceptibility to pain in the joints and muscles, difficulty in breathing, and a heavy feeling in the stomach" (again, p. 103).

Latman (1987), reviewing research up to 1984, observed that links between chronic pain and weather conditions have existed for over a century.[403] Still, because weather variables were poorly defined by early meteo-medical researchers and due to a combination of small sample sizes, case study analyses, and the anecdotal and subjective nature of much of this early work, results are often contradictory insofar as they relate to specific relationships between weather and sensitivity variables, beyond pointing to a general relationship between weather sensitivity and pain. Other, albeit unfortunately older work–from 1992, 1986, 1990, and 1987 respectively–has suggested that as many as 97% of people with nonmalignant chronic pain,[404] 69% of people with rheumatoid arthritis,[405] and 83% of those with osteoarthritis[406] self-identify as "weather sensitive." Thorough research of this nature tends to be highly specialized and relatively rare.

One study found weather changes to be the most attributed cause, outside of psychological distress, of symptom flares for individuals with rheumatoid arthritis.[407] Cooler temperatures and high atmospheric pressure and humidity levels appear accepted in association with pain in rheumatoid arthritis and chronic pain conditions,[408-412] and coolness and high pressure are widely accepted triggers for fibromyalgia flare-ups.[408] A bit of a contradiction to the above temperature-arthritis link is that *decreases* in atmospheric pressure sometimes induce joint pain (*if* one distinguishes subclinical joint pain from *diagnosable* arthritis and fibromyalgia–this fits intuitions that storms and fronts induce pain).[412] Weather-related physical pain appears unrelated to regional climate regimes.[409,410]

Other research in this area examines beliefs about weather-induced physical pain. While most chronically-affected people tend to believe weather affects their pain levels,[411] researchers observe that although higher degrees of weather sensitivity *are* associated with higher levels of functional impairment and psychological distress in people with fibromyalgia, a greater association seems to exist between self-reported beliefs in weather-induced pain and physical sensitivity than actually-measured, objective pain and sensitivity.[413]

The majority of people with rheumatoid arthritis believe themselves negatively affected by weather, particularly low temperatures and in times of high or increasing humidity,[413-416] although individuals with fibromyalgia appear to report weather-related sensitivities more often or consistently than those with rheumatoid arthritis.[414]

* * *

A study[417] published in 2005, with nationally-representative samples of German and Canadian residents, extrapolated that 54.5% of German residents and 61% of Canadians consider themselves physically sensitive to weather conditions. Adults aged 60 or older were the most sensitive in both groups–a finding replicated in other European research.[418]

German participants reported sensitivity to storminess and cold weather while Canadian participants reported sensitivities to cold weather, damp (but not rainy) conditions, and rain.[417] The most frequent symptoms reported in Germany were headache/migraine, lethargy, sleep disturbance, fatigue, joint pain, irritation, depression, vertigo, lack of mental concentration, and scar pain. Canadians most reported colds; psychological effects; and painful joints, muscles, or arthritis.[417] These results add validity to the notion of meteoropathy. Readers should note these findings reflect interviews conducted in 1994 (Germany) and 2001 (Canada). Elsewhere in this literature, we find that older individuals' greater levels of physical weather sensitivity often dictate their outdoor exercise regimen.[419,420]

* * *

Meanwhile, in a more strictly medical context than the above findings, there is evidence to suggest that sharp declines in atmospheric pressure are associated with an induction of labor in some pregnant women,[421-423] and childbirth prematurity.[424] One older study (1984) suggested (with statistical significance beyond chance) that onset of labor is as much as 34% more likely on winter days with low pressure, temperatures notably lower than the day before, and high wind speeds, and above average during the 48 hours before and after the passage of cold fronts, especially so in the 12 hours prior to the front's arrival.[423]

Social-Cognitive Psychologies of Climate Change

Climate psychology, while newly popular, is an extensive topic. Its breadth challenged me in determining the discussion's focal range. Hence, my aim is to briefly summarize some of the issues driving ongoing dialogue around climate change, with emphasis on the role of the news media and social activism in framing climate matters, and the social and cognitive psychological bases of climate perception.

Since the days of Galileo and Ptolemy; Isaac Newton; and, more recently, the likes of Marie Curie, Albert Einstein, and Rosalind Franklin, science has pursued truth (or falsification of non-truths). Innately curious scientists have traditionally sought to conceptualize and organize sets of related observations to explain the world in terms of scientific laws.[425-427] These are subsequently maintained by overarching norms and principles around the process of "doing science." Ideally, they foster healthy, open-minded skepticism which drives systematic questioning of one's own, and others', findings in order to provide alternate explanations that are more logical, precise, and accurate for evolving situations and contexts.

Comprising difficult work on par with the sciences of weather and mood, weather and health, and weather-risk decision-making, the research literature on climate messaging and perception is filled with conflicting results and competing hypotheses. These are intersectionally psychological–each individual holds biases, beliefs, and perceptions–and sociological–each person attaches to an ideology, tribe, or side and/ or opinion or viewpoint, and is situated within a wider context. Some people are skeptics or outright deniers of the consensus science. There are those proclaiming the end-of-times; who are apathetic with little to no belief in society's ability to positively affect future outcomes; or who are motivated by potential profits (financially, professionally, and otherwise). My response? I have no interest in politicizing or weaponizing science and support the open, dispassionate reporting of empirical findings as well as critical evaluation of available evidence. What follows is my best attempt at navigating a broad slice of the climate science literature.

Climate Messaging and the News Media

Significant environmental impacts of climate change are presently unfolding and a worsening future global condition is predicted. The need for swift and effective climate action is inarguable. Activists like Greta Thunberg, who has become a spokesperson[428,429] for climate messaging, are absolutely correct: We are in a time of climate emergency and environmental crisis.

The saying goes "No news is good news" but maybe it should be "Good news is no news." We humans seem to have an innate preference for negative, over positive, attribution,[430-435] and people correspondingly tend to pay more attention and give more weight to bad news than good.[436-438] This negativity bias, as psychologists call it, contributes to a preponderance of gloomy stories the world over.[439]

In response to declarations, framings, and concerns of climate emergency, there has been extensive research into conceptual representations of climate, both visually and linguistically (metaphors, strategies, frames, and narratives) so that scientists and media and other communicators can transform largely invisible, conceptual ideas into visible, concrete forms. A 2018 review[440] by Wang, Corner, Chapman, and Markowitz focused on visual media representations of climate and climate change across the digital landscape, including social media, online news, and video-based channels such as film and television. Perhaps the most striking finding was that excepting what is a decidedly background-contextual exhibition, little to no visual messaging focuses on the impacts climate change brings to real people. When humans are depicted, it is (in order from greatest-least) politicians, public figures, protesters, and scientists who are shown; there is an overwhelming absence of genuinely *human* stories in these visual representations

Instead, the consequences of climate change on the physical environment are the most prominent aspect conveyed through visual messaging.[440] Typically, these depictions are figurative, making use of stylized infographics and graphs rather than actual photographs. Photographs–generally of the fossil fuels industry, including smokestacks, mass transport, and deforestation–meanwhile, tend to portray the causes of climate in order to evoke a certain (presumably political) emotional percept. Wang and colleagues observed (p. 98) "there are so far no analyses of images that link other individual actions (consumer-driven electronics, fashion, household energy use) with wider societal and climate change-related impacts," and that climate change reporting focuses very little on solutions-focused imagery (including mitigating and adaptive technology, and renewable energy elements).[440] The review brings these and other important matters into focus and makes recommendations by which climate communicators can remediate such shortcomings.

A 2010 review by Nerlich, Koteyko, and Brown provided in-depth discussion on the ways media coverage and linguistic conceptualizations have morphed and intertwined in the communication of climate information.[441] It is especially noteworthy (and likely against many individuals' prior conceptions), that in light of the aforementioned evidence for negativity biases and the differing beliefs about climate change people possess, the journalistic norm of balanced reporting on climate change in the *New York Times*, *Washington Post*, *Los Angeles Times*, and *Wall Street Journal* from 1988-2002, and in the United States and United Kingdom more broadly from 2003-2006, actually led to coverage biased *against* the then-emerging scientific consensus on climate change.[442-446] As Boykoff and Boykoff (p. 125) put it,[431] "[t]he continuous juggling act journalists engage in, [sic] often mitigates against meaningful, accurate, and urgent coverage of the issue of global warming."

Related to this is that although the news media plays on emotions in a variety of ways, it is not necessarily always with negative outcome.[447-451] This section closes with a mention that although many have felt the need for caution due to the negativity and polarization associated with climate topics,[452,453] broadcast meteorologists have recently joined the climate education party[454-456] as their views on climate change have shifted.[457]

One multi-year study conducted from 2015-2017[455,[21]] examined data from 1,575 participants to determine the information reported by broadcast meteorologists interested in communicating to viewers about climate change. Over half (56%) who indicated interest in reporting about climate change pointed to the use of historical climatology data as their format-of-choice, as opposed to information about climate change impacts, adaptation efforts, protective behaviors, mitigation efforts, and future projections. Over half (57.9%) used multiple modes of communication (social media, 42.7%; school visits; 36.3%; community events, 33.1%; on-air broadcasts, 31.3%) to get their messages out to viewers and other community members, and most (61.9%) had received positive feedback on their reporting from viewers.[455]

Concerns About Climate Change Apathy; and the Role of Social Activism

While climate journalism has historically been balanced, negativity bias interjected into climate change (and more general) news does shape collective understanding of world events. A natural symptom of scientific facts about climate change alone not selling stories or prompting action,[458] more partisan news outlets sometimes juxtapose factual coverage and cloud the perceptual skies by both emoting about and pseudo-intellectualizing climate change–think more entertainment-based, "talking head" than scientific discourse–in order to elicit views and responses. At worst, data are cherry-picked or framed in such a way as to send a certain message. What has resulted is an apparent proliferation of increasingly dire, distressing messages and, helped along by social media, the perception that climate coverage is biased across the mass media landscape.

As I see it, these messages are doing little to promote social action and change. Concerned with mental health, especially related to natural disasters, I worry the constant vocal messaging around climate change in combination with societal factors that limit effective action are driving, and will continue to drive, many people to a state of counterproductive anxiety and motivated apathy for climate change discussion and action. Moser (2007),[458] Lertzman (2017),[459] and Schinko (2020)[460] provide more critical analyses. Anecdotally, much of this apathy and avoidance ensues because climate change is of less or no concern for people who cannot meet their basic needs of living–even within the USA and other wealthy countries.

This position is not new: Although not without contention and debate,[461] it has, in fact, long been argued that environmental concern is collectively predicated on the strength and health of our personal and collective economies.[109;462-469] More fundamentally, economic security outweighs environmental concern in terms of universal human needs.[470,471]

Abraham Maslow, speaking to the human condition in devising his "hierarchy of needs," theorized (similarly to some First Nation/Blackfoot Indigenous groups) that people innately require adequate access to food, water, shelter, and reproductive capacity; to be secure, stable, and generally free from day-to-day fears; to have friends and supportive family and perhaps a significant other; to have a degree of personal achievement and mastery and to be recognized and respected by others; and to be able to pursue those higher callings whose fulfilment make one the best one can be. [470,471]

People working paycheck-to-paycheck; who are worried about physical or emotional violence, home evictions, foreclosure, the quality of their drinking water, where their next meal will come from, or where they will sleep the next night; who are confronting potentially serious medical conditions either for themselves or with close others; or who are in abusive relationships or otherwise unsafe or unstable living or workplace conditions–all these and many others will not be worried about climate change because they have more pressing and immediate concerns. It is a privilege to be able to worry about and, especially, to act on, climate change. As societal problems of the current era, circa 2020–crime, wealth inequalities, racism, homophobia, transphobia, problematic workplace conditions, lack of adequate and safe living conditions, and the like–continue or worsen, fewer and fewer people will be able to actionally think about and address climate change.

With all these stressors, our "finite pools of worry" (see Weber, 2010)[472] are consumed by attentiveness to economic and material matters rather than wider social and environmental policy issues. Adding aggressive media messaging to this bubbling cauldron of concern creates a sense of inadequacy, hopelessness, and moral and emotional fatigue when people cannot, by virtue of their living situation, do much, if anything, to affect real change. Even localized, personal efforts to live more sustainably are curtailed when one cannot put food on the table. Such lifestyle impacts often understandably limit participation in activism and collective action efforts.

Climate change is everyone's problem, and we all must act, together, to fight it. Activism efforts, including protests, are one part of a political messaging about climate that reflect a very human, visceral reaction. Climate anxiety and ecological grief motivate many into such action (and, of course, so too do business-related profit, genuine altruism and environmental concern, and other factors). Greta Thunberg provides perhaps the most well-known recent illustration of an individual funneling these emotional and cognitive responses into a positive gain.

Thunberg, on the autism spectrum, was deeply affected upon learning of climate change in school.[22] Channeling strengths–including conscientiousness, attention to detail, hyper-focus, a willingness to directly say what needs to be said, and repulsion towards deceit and hypocrisy–she struck out in 2018 to bring attention to climate change through a weekly school strike (using #FridaysForFuture for publicity). This led to even wider local, regional, and global speeches, rallies, and awareness campaigns that galvanized previous climate activism[480-483] and imbued new energy and enthusiasm to a global, all-ages activist movement.[484-494]

In the United States, three forms of adult activism relate to contacting elected representatives, supporting organizations working on climate, and attending climate change rallies or meetings.[480] Among adolescents and teens, another three types of activism have been defined as dutiful, disruptive, and dangerous subtypes of dissent.[490] Dutiful dissent involves working within established economic or political systems; disruptive dissent involves desire to change existing systems; and dangerous dissent, rather than referring to violence, involves developing and initiating new systemic alternatives to inspire and sustain long-term transformations.

Perceptions of Climate Change

As discussed previously, locally-occurring weather events bias perceptions of whether or not the global climate is changing.[96-98] This is one of the fundamental mechanisms driving climate beliefs. A person in Russian Siberia might not believe the climate is changing because their experience is one of frigid weather.[100,101] A person in China, where it is warmer and where pollution runs rampant, might.[103,104] Phenomenological accounts understand well, based on the ways people discern meaning and extrapolate context from personal experience, that a person whose primary experience is of a cooler environment might believe there is no change in temperatures at a more national or international scale. Likewise, it is easy to see how a person with experiences rooted in locales regularly subject to warmer weather patterns will believe in trends of increasing global warmth. All knowledge is personally, subjectively-constructed.[495,496]

I want to add a bit more context to the finding that the availability heuristic contributes to climate perceptions.[347] I mentioned earlier that a lack of experience with the concept of climate change naturally lends portends an inability to recall and then respond to climate-based threats (in my view, because *climate change*-as-concept has not been accurately associated, via framing, with climate change-derived extreme weather events). Consider that people have relatively short-term memories and long periods of particular weather conditions, or repeated experiences with severe and dangerous weather, might influence perceptions of recent change or risk by enhancing emotional recall or perceived intensity of the conditions to which the individual is acclimated. This may, when the individual's regional climate does begin changing, induce perceptions and attitudes that present conditions are the worst "ever."

Frames about climate change versus global warming, which evoke perceptions in the U.K. in a similar manner as in the United States,[319,497] also likely contribute. Similar to associations people have between climate change and flooding, drought, high summer temperatures, and seasonal change,[498,499] they are a part of the climate change attribution process, which is a difficult and controversial area of climate science revolving around whether or not singular extreme weather events can be attributed to Earth's changing climate.[500]

These difficulties are reflected in Capstick and Pidgeon's nationally-representative U.K. study (209 individuals in 39 qualitative focus groups which yielded 5,631 data points; 2014; also see Capstick, 2012)[497,501] where nearly a third of participants did not take a position for or against the attribution of extreme cold weather events to climate change. Still, only a small minority believed the occurrence of cold weather disconfirms the idea that climate change is ongoing.

Capstick and Pidgeon reported,[497] further (pp. 704-705), that "during the winter months immediately preceding the public perceptions research, cold weather events were framed in the media both in terms of evidence contrary to the veracity of climate change, and as evidence of its manifestation." This is just one reason why reporting of accurate news headlines and realistic referencing of climatic time scales ("highest temperatures *on record*" as opposed to "highest temperatures *ever*") is paramount to individuals' discerning what is and is not worthy of concern, and fully comprehending and responding to those climate threats that do exist. Anecdotal observation reveals all too often that "ever" is used to emotively transform climate headlines when "on record" is more appropriate. "Ever" presumes to know the state of the Earth before reliable record-keeping existed, and in keeping with good scientific practice it is folly to presume that even the best numerical simulation models are 100% accurate.

Moving back to more concrete discussion, research suggests women worry more than men about climate change and that worry about climate change is not associated with singular experiences of severe and dangerous weather resulting in property damage or injury.[206] Furthermore, cultural ties and desire to conform with the beliefs and values of one's in-group contribute to perceptions of and attitudes towards climate change. Although it has come under reasonable criticism,[502] it is worth mentioning that within cultural cognition theory,[503,504] Kahan proposed that public disagreement over societal issues–including, but not limited to climate change–ensues not due to lack of informational comprehension, but rather because people "endorse whichever position reinforces their connection to others with whom they share important ties" (p. 296).[503]

In other words, some people perceive risk based partially on their values, and attempts to remain congruent with these can impact whether action is taken to mitigate the known and projected effects of climate change. Kahan further posited "identity-protective cognition" as a means by which people assimilate risk information.[503;505,506] This process is a form of motivated reasoning, driving people to align with beliefs and values that are congruent with the primary views of their in-groups so as to protect their cultural identities. In other words, when people–who, with their innate need to belong–are exposed to scientific information, their culturally-biased cognitive stance and worldview will reinforce and increase their polarization with out-groups that hold opposing values on the issue at hand.[507]

For those leaning egalitarian-collectivist, who believe all people are equal and deserve equal rights and opportunities, the existential threats to health and safety posed to others by climate change enhance environmentalism. Individualists–who favor self-reliance–are in contrast concerned about threats to their freedoms posed by government climate policies.[508] Individualists tend to doubt and disbelieve the climate is changing. Available evidence shows a similar pattern of results in China as in the USA (and one would expect it to hold for other collectivist countries as well).[104]

A 2019 study into the climate change activism practices of Latino/a Americans found them more likely than White-Americans to report having contacted a government official in the past and were more likely to report future intentions to do so. Significantly greater degrees of risk perception, an egalitarian/collectivist worldview, pro-environmental cultural norms, collective political efficacy belief, and a greater tendency to discuss climate change in one's social network predicted these relationships.[494]

With all this in mind, one can begin to see how vital political orientation and ideology and cultural values are to the formation of climate change beliefs. On the basis of political party, United States Democrats have tended to more favorably support environmental issues than Republicans. Still, even with the historical individualism within the country,[509] USA environmental issues have tended to be a non-partisan matter. Both parties have on the average been, if not fairly cooperative, at least single-mindedly supportive on this issue (these references–Dunlap and McCright, 2008, in particular–provide thorough review).[510-512]

Climate change beliefs are at present becoming increasingly polarized due to shifts among conservatives towards political policy which favors enhanced de-regulation and withdrawal of governmental oversight of the environment,[512] and the liberal desire for more government controls. Closely related to this divide are beliefs and attitudes towards climate activism–people split along party lines with Democrats more favorable and Republicans less.[513] I recommend Dunlap, McCright, and Yarosh;[514] Guber;[515] and Schuldt and Roh[319] for a comprehensive political-climate scientific review.

Although research[516] has suggested scientists and non-scientists conceptualize and approach climate activism from vastly different angles–scientists tend to lean towards rationality and rigidity in their views while non-scientists trend more reflexive and less abstract and cautious–the winds of change are blowing at gale-force speed, loosening scientists' historically neutral view on such political matters and inducing them to become more involved.[23]

Cross-national Perceptions of Earth's Changing Climate

In 2015, Lee, Markowitz, Howe, Ko, and Leiserowitz published[110] the results of an expansive, multinational study they conducted across 119 countries to begin determining what might be some global predictors of climate change awareness and risk perception.

They implicate general educational attainment as the single strongest predictor of climate change awareness at the global scale, while understanding about causal mechanisms of climate change is the strongest predictor of climate-related risk perception, especially among those in Latin America and Europe. Perception of local temperature change is the strongest predictor of climate-risk perception for much of Africa and also across many Asian nations. In the U.S., climate change awareness is most strongly related to civic engagement, media access, and achieved education. American participants with greater civic engagement were almost always aware of climate change while less civically-active participants, and those with less access to the media, tended to be more unaware.[110]

Lee and colleagues' work underscores the role of politics in shaping American perceptions of climate change. The strongest predictors of climate change risk perception among American participants in the study–in line with other research presented here–are (1) beliefs about the causal mechanisms of climate change; (2) perceptions of changes in local temperature; and (3) attitudes towards government-sponsored endeavors to protect and preserve the environment.[110]

Furthermore, the perceived risks of climate change are lower among Americans who believe climate change is a naturally-occurring process; determine that average local temperatures are becoming colder or staying the same;[97,98,110] and show satisfaction with environmental preservation efforts. In contrast, education, geography (living in an urban, versus rural, area), and household income drive climate change awareness in China, where lower-income, less-educated individuals living rurally were least aware.[110] This is consistent with Dai, Kesternich, Löschel, and Ziegler's 2015 study mentioned earlier.[103]

A comprehensive review[520] of climate change and global warming perception research dating back to the 1980s, by Capstick, Whitmarsh, Poortinga, Pidgeon, and Upham in 2015, supported the conclusion that many of these perceptions are at least somewhat temporally stable, and highlighted the role played by political lobbying and psychological and wider sociocultural factors in their development. Capstick and colleagues suggest confirmation bias–searching for, interpreting, recalling information in a way that confirms one's pre-existing beliefs–is increasingly problematic with implications for increasing skepticism towards climate science.[521]

Capstick and colleagues also discuss, among other topics, the idea of climate fatigue, about which I expressed concern earlier. To summarize the review is beyond my aim here, however; I recommend it as a deep-dive into many of the psychological and, especially, sociological and political, factors of this topic, for anyone interested in further learning. Hornsey, Harris, Bain, and Fielding (2016) provide a similar, strong review,[522] while McDonald, Chai, and Newell (2015) extensively explore the intersect of personal experience and psychological distance from climate change.[523]

* * *

Hopefully, this section has highlighted some of the complexities existing at the intersection of psychological science, communication, and climate. All of this research shows that depictions of climate change matter, just as much as the framing of more immediate, moment-to-moment weather messages. Crucially, it is what we choose to do with all this information that will help decide the ultimate impact of climate change.

What's Next in
Weather and Climate
Psychology?

Now that we have covered numerous–but certainly not all–topics on our road trip through the domain of weather-related psychology, you and I are faced with a compelling question: What comes next in weather-climate psychology? There is no easy answer, for the scientific and operational landscapes are ever-shifting. New scholarship is constantly published and new paradigms of practice frequently introduced. Changes on the broad weather-social science horizon are fluid like weather itself, their outcomes even less predictable. Still, there are a few areas upon which I want to shine a light, where future efforts would or could prove fruitful.

One deals with vulnerable populations–weather communication to and with individuals who, for example, have cognitive or color processing differences; are physically disabled; Deaf; hard-of-hearing; blind or with low vision beyond the use of corrective lenses or surgeries; or are affected by different socioeconomic factors (such as being homeless or a single, low-income parent). I included some of the advocacy and empirical work I've done with weather communication and colorblindness, and weather salience and autism, and as mentioned various weather enterprise professionals are expanding into work with those who are Deaf, hard-of-hearing, blind and low-vision, and physically disabled.[362] Still, this area is understudied given the percentage of the population these groups comprise.

Next, given its centrality and utility to weather-social science as, potentially, a moderator or mediator which can explain other variables, weather salience remains understudied. Perceptual and epistemic, or sensory- and information-based, curiosities for weather are two strong candidates to further work here. I have done some initial work on epistemic weather curiosity[524] while Alan Stewart has established the measurement of perceptual weather curiosity.[525]

Still another area–that is burgeoning and one of my favorite topics–concerns human factors research into the personal and professional functioning of meteorologists and meteorologist-adjacent emergency management professionals. I briefly mentioned a line of research focused on revealing the evolving climate change beliefs and education-related efforts of broadcast meteorologists. Elsewhere, work into meteorological workplace processes is growing. NWS meteorologists, academics, and others collaborate on field research centered around better understanding forecaster job performance and are increasingly interested in the ways meteorologists process and use the firehose of information with which they contend.[240,526-532] Other research has begun looking more closely at the ways emergency managers comprehend, use, and communicate weather information.[533-542]

I, for my part, have examined meteorologist mental health and personality tendencies in two studies.[543,544] The first compared meteorologists with engineers and physicists in order to test a separate cognitive style hypothesis relating to autism (and found that meteorologists score highly on a test of autistic-like traits, on par with engineers and physicists–groups in whom links to autism have been well-established). The meteorologists were less stressed, depressed, and anxious, and more extraverted, conscientious, and agreeable than the engineers and physicists.

In the second study, focused exclusively on the meteorological field,[544] broadcast meteorologists were most burnt-out at work and in their personal lives, were higher in extraversion, and also the most anxious; NWS meteorologists were most burnt-out working with partners across the weather enterprise. A mixed grouping of academic, private sector, military, and non-NWS operational meteorologists were more agreeable and had greater job satisfaction than the broadcast and NWS meteorologists; meanwhile, there were no differences in test scores for grit, life satisfaction, self-concept clarity, happiness, stress, or depression, suggesting a relatively uniform distribution of these traits. I am currently lead-authoring a paper on the workplace, weather-related trauma-coping strategies of meteorologists and emergency managers while conducting a study into the effects of childhood life experiences on adult personality and mental health tendencies in meteorologists, for comparison with the general population.

* * *

Looking forward, I confidently forecast that weather-social communication models, theories, and operationalized practice strategies will continue blossoming. Research into behavioral reactions to, attitudes towards, and perceptions of severe and dangerous weather will also continue in earnest, and climate change messaging, attitudes, and behavioral response research will flourish. Myriad efforts will continue and, hopefully, even more topic integrations will arise than I have showcased here. I would love to see neuroscientific work–eye-tracking and brain-imaging–as well as research taking advantage of wearable devices and increasing mobile technological capacities for human physiological measurement. I hope, also, that the National Weather Service will integrate more specific psychological principles into operations.

Encouragingly, psychologists and meteorologists increasingly recognize the benefits of collaboration. Interdisciplinary weather-social work at the University of Oklahoma, for example, now often involves psychologists as well as meteorologists, geographers, anthropologists, communication practitioners, and others. Psychologists, furthermore, are beginning to propose ways in which they can contribute to interdisciplinary work with emergency managers.[545] Hopefully weather enterprise professionals will listen and be open to collaboration.

It is with great interest and excitement that I look forward to witnessing, and hopefully contributing to some of, these many different endeavors and areas in the years to come.

Notes

Preface

[1] Consider, for example, the relatively recent invention of weather observing tools, Luke Howard's classification of clouds,[3] the study of vortex dynamics by Helmholtz[4] and others,[5] Bjerknes' Norwegian Cyclone Model,[6] and the first successful tornado forecast on March 25th, 1948.[7]

Weather in Everyday Life

[2] The term for this art of seeing shapes in the clouds is nephellococcygia. It comes from *The Birds* (414 BC), a play by Aristophanes (446-386 BC).

[3] See Stanley Gedzelman's *The Meteorological Odyssey of Vincent Van Gogh*,[29] and Catherine Dunlop's *Looking at the Wind: Paintings of the Mistral in Fin-de-Siècle France*[30] for two interesting analyses at the intersection of art and weather.

[4] A revolutionary film effect for the time, Dorothy's famous tornado was created with a large sock! See https://www.washingtonpost.com/news/capital-weather-gang/wp/2014/08/15/its-a-twister-75-years-later-wizard-of-oz-is-still-a-tornado-classic/

[5] See insert A2.2 at https://www.ipcc.ch/sr15/chapter/spm/

[6] In the survey of 2,251 nationally-representative individuals, there were two groups of respondents: Those who followed their local news closely and those who did not. In the follow-closely group, 92% of respondents reported weather as the topic considered most important. This finding was the same for the group who did not follow news closely, with 82% reporting weather as their most important topic. Breaking news, politics, crime, and education followed to round out the top 5 for those who followed news closely; for the non-close group, it was breaking news, politics and a category for general business happenings, crime, and arts and culture.

[7] Note: As of December 4th, 2020. Search term popularity can be explored at https://trends.google.com/trends/explore?date=all&q=weather

[8] For further reading about childhood developmental processes, an accessible book is *Inventing Ourselves: The Secret Life of the Teenage Brain*, by neuroscientist Sarah-Jayne Blakemore. For further discussion of this study, the authors have posted a number of online blog entries, including one that

hypothesizes about the possible effects of these findings on youth-led, and other, climate change activism. See https://findingnature.org.uk/2019/06/12/teenage-dip/ and https://findingnature.org.uk/2019/09/29/climate-strikes/

[9] Socially-desirable responding is a common response bias and problem in self-report research, where people attempt to respond in ways seen as favorable by others rather than truthfully. Here, the researchers measured and accounted for various types of socially-desirable responding in their statistical model, meaning the findings persisted even as people were deceptive.

[10] It's worth pointing out this study by Sims and Baumann is from 1972. More recent work (2018) has investigated fatalism with respect to the receipt and processing of nighttime tornado warnings in Tennessee,[89] and with respect to earthquake messaging.[90] Cohen and Nisbett,[91] however, in 1998, contradicted these results by finding no differences in fatalism for the perceived riskiness of various health practices when comparing Southern to Midwestern residents. Though one could argue these are totally disparate contexts, results for this line of work appear mixed since fatalism is a trait-based individual difference; this specific result may depend on contextual, temporal, and cultural as well as measurement factors.

Effects of Weather and Climate on Mental Health

[11] Of course, you should always consult your primary care doctor before taking any medication or supplement, and work with a trained psychotherapist or psychiatrist when taking more than simple self-help steps to improve your mental health.

[12] For more on this neural circuitry, see Schmidt and Kofuji's 2008 paper *Novel Insights into Non-Image Forming Visual Processing in the Retina*.[185] Carlson and Birkett[153] also provide a solid, if often technical, foundation on the neurophysiology of the human visual system more generally.

Weather-related Decision-Making

[13] Meteorologist readers will be familiar with internal aspects of the forecasting process discussed next, if not the statistics presented. I hope those who are familiar will forgive my relatively simple treatment of the topic. My goal is only to provide a basic overview to spark further study. This section was written with thanks to James Aydelot, Benjamin Cathay, Rob Dale, and Joe Ripberger for assistance in tracking down a number of referenced studies.

[14] For this reason, the NWS Hazard Simplification (HazSimp) initiative (https://www.weather.gov/hazardsimplification/) has for several years sought to better understand both weather enterprise-internal, and general public, perceptions of watches, warnings, and advisories so that they can be communicated more effectively and efficiently.

[15] In pre-post surveys, participants respond to the same types of items (e.g., trait anxiety) at multiple time points in order to assess how the effects of different interventions or stimuli impact their scores. Here, risk perception-based questionnaires were completed before and after exposure to a hazard warning message.

Framing and Adapting to Weather

[16] When the participants were instructed to make decisions about closing schools based on snow accumulation forecasts, the consistency and accuracy of the forecasts were systematically changed so that some participants randomly received one presentation and others received another.

[17] That is, as people thought more intuitively, the other variable also increased. For those unfamiliar, in correlation, a positive relationship is one in which both variables increase or decrease together. A negative relationship is one in which one variable increases while the other decreases. Correlation simply indicates a statistical relationship exists; it cannot be used to infer that one variable caused another's outcome.

Weather and Political Voting Behavior

[18] See also, for example, the 1966 work of William Andrews,[382] and of Gomez, Hansford, and Krause more recently (2007).[383]

[19] Also note that Gomez, Hansford, and Krause identified several methodological issues with the Kentucky study by Gatrell and Bierly, a previous study by Knack,[387] and a study by Shachar and Nalebuff.[388] The most significant of their criticisms were that Gatrell and Bierly excluded essential variables in their statistical model, which could have led to spurious results, and that Shachar and Nalebuff's rainfall estimation measure was biased.

[20] This 2011 study analyzed weather conditions and voter turnout in over 400 municipalities from 1971-2010. The authors did not report, however, at what point temperature increases would begin to negatively impact voter turnout. As they did not provide any data visualizations, it is unclear if their data reflected such a point. It seems most prudent to presume there would be such an inverted U-curve associated with data of this nature.

Social-Cognitive Psychologies of Climate Change

[21] Note that the authors report having "conducted on-line surveys with every person currently working in weathercasting and broadcast meteorology in the United States" (Timm et al., 2020, p. E131). Rather, they only *sent* their survey to every broadcast meteorologist annually and did not *receive* responses from all these potential recipients. Response rates of 22.6% (2015, n = 466), 31.2% (2016, n = 629), and 22.1% (2017, n = 480), for a total sample size of 1,575, were instead achieved by their recruitment effort. Participant pool members who do not contribute a usable amount of data–and the majority of those contacted here did not take part–are not typically counted towards sample sizes.

[22] It has long been known that people on the autism spectrum are highly passionate about different topics,[473-478] including the natural world. In fact, Thunberg is joined in her activism efforts by others on the spectrum, including Dara McAnulty and Chris Packham. Temple Grandin, meanwhile, was spurred by a love of animals to design more humane equipment for the livestock industry;[479] and I myself am autistic (and think this book speaks for itself as to my interest on these matters–WINK!).

[23] While various statements by the American Meteorological Society, American Geophysical Union, and other meteorologically-inclined entities are well-known, I want to bring to readers' attention to a recent (2018) statement by the American Psychological Association, calling on psychologists to take action on climate change,[517] and similar take-action messages by individual psychologists.[518,519]

References

1. De Figueiredo Neves, G. Z., Gallardo, N. P., & da Silva Vecchia, F. A. (2017). A short critical history on the development of meteorology and climatology. *Climate*, *5*(1), 23.

2. Jankovic, V. (2006). The end of classical meteorology, c. 1800. In G. J. H. McCall, A. J. Bowden, & R. J. Howarth (Eds.), *The history of meteoritics and key meteorite collections: Fireballs, falls and finds* (pp. 91-99). Geological Society of London.

3. Howard, L. (1803). *On the modification of clouds*. John Churchill and Sons.

4. Helmholtz, H. (1858). Über Integrale der hydrodynamischen Gleichungen, welche den Wirbelbewegungen entsprechen. *Journal für die reine und angewandte Mathematik, 55*, 25–55.

5. Meleshko, V. V., & Aref, H. (2007). A bibliography of vortex dynamics 1858-1956. In E. van Giessen & H. Aref, (Eds.), *Advances in applied mechanics*. Elsevier.

6. Bjerknes, V. (1921). On the dynamics of the circular vortex: With applications to the atmosphere and atmospheric vortex and wave motions. *Geofysiske Publikationer*, *2*(4).

7. Grice, G. K., Trapp, R. J., Corfidi, S. F., Davies-Jones, R., Buonanno, C. C., Craven, J. P., Droegemeier, K. K., Duchon, C., Houghton, J. V., Prentice, R. A., Romine, G., Schlacter, K., & Wagner, K. K. (1999). The golden anniversary celebration of the first tornado forecast. *Bulletin of the American Meteorological Society*, *80*(7), 1341–1348.

8. Laskin, D. (2004). *The children's blizzard*. HarperCollins Publishers.

9. Larson, E. (2000). *Isaac's storm: A man, a time, and the deadliest hurricane in history*. Random House.

10. Stewart, S., & Livingston, P. (2013, November 20 and November 26). *The great storm of 1913 remembered (Parts 1 and 2).* Michigan State University Extension.

11. McDonald, W. F. (1935). The hurricane of August 31 to September 6, 1935. *Monthly Weather Review, 63*(9), 269–271.

12. Boyack, K. W., Klavans, R., & Börner, K. (2005). Mapping the background of science. *Scientometrics, 64*(3), 351–374.

13. Kazdin, A. E. (Ed). (2000). Personality psychology. *Encyclopedia of psychology.* American Psychological Association.

14. Ventimiglia, J. C., & DiRenzo, G. J. (1982). Sociological conceptions of personality. *Social Behavior and Personality, 10*(1), 25–37.

15. Peek, L., & Stough, L. M. (2010). Children with disabilities in the context of disaster: A social vulnerability perspective. *Child Development, 81*(4), 1260–1270.

16. Losee, J. E., Smith, C. T, & Webster, G. D. (2020). Politics, personality and impulsivity can color people's perceptions of–and responses to–hurricane threats of varying severity. *Personality and Social Psychology Bulletin*, early online release.

17. National Academies of Sciences, Engineering, and Medicine. (2018). *Integrating social and behavioral sciences within the weather enterprise*. The National Academies Press.

18. Gruntfest, E. (2018). *Weather and society: Toward integrated approaches*. Wiley-Blackwell.

19. Harley, T. A. (2018). *The psychology of weather*. Routledge.

20. Beattie, G., & McGuire, L. (2018). *The psychology of climate*. Routledge.

21. Daipha, P. (2015). *Masters of uncertainty: Weather forecasters and the quest for ground truth*. The University of Chicago Press.

22. Hoffman, R. R., LaDue, D. S., Mogil, H. M., Roebber, P. J., & Trafton, G. (2017). *Minding the weather: How expert forecasters think*. MIT Press.

23. Dodds, J. (2011). *Psychoanalysis and ecology at the edge of chaos: Complexity theory, Deleuze, Gauttari and psychoanalysis for a climate in crisis*. Routledge.

24. Weintrobe, S. (Ed.). (2012). *Engaging with climate change: Psychoanalytic and interdisciplinary perspectives*. Routledge.

25. Orange, D. M. (2016). *Climate crisis, psychoanalysis, and radical ethics*. Routledge.

26. Hogget, P. (Ed.). (2019). *Climate psychology: On indifference to disaster*. Palgrave MacMillan.

27. Zimmerman, L. (2020). *Trauma and the discourse of climate change*. Routledge.

28. Mathers, D. (Ed.). *Depth psychology and climate change: The green book*. Routledge.

29. Gedzelman, S. D. (1990). The meteorological odyssey of Vincent Van Gogh. *Leonardo, 23*(1), 107–116.

30. Dunlop, C. (2015). Looking at the wind: Paintings of the Mistral in Fin-de-Siècle France. *Environmental History*, *20*(3), 505–518.

31. Intergovernmental Panel on Climate Change. (2007). *AR4 climate change 2007: Synthesis report.*

32. Intergovernmental Panel on Climate Change. (2013*). Climate change 2013: The physical science basis.*

33. Intergovernmental Panel on Climate Change. (2018). *Special report: Global warming of 1.5 °C.*

34. Wolf, J., & Moser, S. C. (2011). Individual understandings, perceptions, and engagement with climate change: Insights from in-depth studies across the world. *Wiley Interdisciplinary Reviews: Climate*, *2*(4), 547–569.

35. Whitmarsh, L. (2009). What's in a name? Commonalities and differences in public understanding of "climate change" and "global warming." *Public Understanding of Science*, *18*, 401–420.

36. Allen, D. E., McAleer, M., & Reid, D. M. (2018). Fake news and indifference to scientific fact: President Trump's confused tweets on global warming, climate change and weather. Universidad Complutense Working Paper #1817.

37. Miller, C., Purcell, K., & Rosenstiel, T. (2012, April 12). *72% of Americans follow local news closely*. Pew Research Center.

38. Zion, L. (2017, July 28). *Better than sex? Why we are so obsessed with the weather*. The Guardian.

39. Maddern, C., & Jenner, D. (2009). *Public user survey – summer 2009. A report of research findings*. World Meteorological Organization.

40. U.K. Met Office. (2015, August 14). *Met Office releases new research looking at the UK's obsession with the weather*.

41. D.A. (1983). *Some observations on mental models*. In D. Gentner, & A. L. Stevens, (Eds.), *Mental models* (pp. 7-14). Erlbaum.

42. Stewart, A. E. (2009). Minding the weather: The measurement of weather salience. *Bulletin of the American Meteorological Society, 90*(12), 1833–1842.

43. Stewart, A. E., Lazo, J. K., Morss, R. E., & Demuth, J. L. (2012). The relationship of weather salience with the perceptions and uses of weather information in a nationwide sample of the United States. *Weather, Climate, and Society, 4*(3), 172–189.

44. Bolton, M. J., Blumberg, W. G., Ault, L. K, Mogil, H. M., & Hanes, S. H. (2020). Initial evidence for increased weather salience in autism spectrum conditions. *Weather, Climate, and Society, 12*(2), 293–307.

45. Bolton, M. J., Mogil, H. M., & Ault, L. K. (2020). An exploratory, preliminary report on United States weather education trends and general population links between weather salience and systemizing. *Journal of Operational Meteorology, 8*(4), 54–63.

46. Zeyer, A., Bölsterli, K., Brovelli, D., & Odermatt, F. (2012). Brain type or sex differences? A structural equation model of the relation between brain type, sex, and motivation to learn science. *International Journal of Science Education*, *34*(5), 779–802.

47. Williams, C. A., Miller, P. W., Black, A. W., & Knox, J. A. (2017). Throwing caution to the wind: National Weather Service wind products as perceived by a weather-salient sample. *Journal of Operational Meteorology*, *5*(9), 103–120.

48. Ballew, M. T., & Omoto, A. M. (2018). Absorption: How nature experiences promote awe and other positive emotions. *Ecopsychology*, *10*(1), 26–35.

49. Cleary, A., Fielding, K. S., Murray, Z., & Roiko, A. (2020). Predictors of nature connection among urban residents: Assessing the role of childhood and adult nature experiences. *Environment and Behavior*, *52*(6), 579–610.

50. Mayer, F. S., & Frantz, C. M. (2004). The Connectedness to Nature Scale: A measure of individuals' feeling in community with nature. *Journal of Environmental Psychology, 24*, 503–515.

51. Nisbet, E. K. L., Zelenski, J. M., and Murphy, S. A. (2009). The nature relatedness scale: Linking individuals' connection with nature to environmental concern and behavior. *Environment and Behavior. 41*, 715–740.

52. Nisbet, E. K., & Zelenski, J. M. (2013). The NR-6: A new brief measure of nature relatedness. *Frontiers in Psychology, 4*, 813.

53. Richardson, M., Hunt, A., Hinds, J., Bragg, R., Fido, D., Petronzi, D., Barbett, L., Clitherow, T., & White, M. (2019). A measure of nature connectedness for children and adults: Validation, performance, and insights. *Sustainability, 11*(12), 3250.

54. Anderson, D. (2019). *Connectedness to nature and pro-environmental behaviour from early adolescence to adulthood: A comparison of urban and rural Canada.* Unpublished Master's thesis, Wilfrid Laurier University.

55. Krettenauer, T., Wang, W., Jia, F., & Yao, Y. (2020). Connectedness with nature and the decline of pro-environmental behavior in adolescence: A comparison of Canada and China. *Journal of Environmental Behavior*, *71*, 101348.

56. Capaldi, C. A., Dopko, R. L., & Zelenski, J. M. (2014). The relationship between nature connectedness and happiness: A meta-analysis. *Frontiers in Psychology*, *5*, 976.

57. Howell, A. J., Dopko, R. L., Passmore, H.-A., & Buro, K. (2011). Nature connectedness: Associations with well-being and mindfulness. *Personality and Individual Differences*, *51*, 166–171.

58. Pereira, M., & Forster, P. (2015). The relationship between connectedness to nature, environmental values, and pro-environmental behaviours. *Reinvention: An International Journal of Undergraduate Research*, *8*(2).

59. Howell, A. J., Passmore, H.-A., & Buro, K. (2013). Meaning in nature: Meaning in life as a mediator of the relationship between nature connectedness and well-being. *Journal of Happiness Studies, 14,* 1681–1696.

60. Pritchard, A., Richardson, M., Sheffield, D., & McEwan, K. (2020). The relationship between nature connectedness and eudaimonic well-being: A meta-analysis. *Journal of Happiness Studies, 21,* 1145–1167.

61. Leary, M. R. (2019). Hypo-egoic identity, prejudice, and intergroup relations. *TPM: Testing, Psychometrics, Methodology in Applied Psychology, 26*(3), 335–346.

62. Martin, L., White, M. P., Hunt, A., Richardson, M., Pahl, S., & Burt, J. (2020). Nature contact, nature connectedness and associations with health, well-being and pro-environmental behaviours. *Journal of Environmental Psychology, 68,* 101389.

63. Richardson, M., & McEwan, K. (2018).
30 Days Wild and the relationships between engagement with nature's beauty,
nature connectedness and well-being.
Frontiers in Psychology, 9, 1500.

64. Kurth, A. M., Narvaez, D., Kohn, R., &
Bae, A. (2020). Indigenous nature connection: A 3-week intervention increased
ecological attachment. *Ecopsychology,
12*(2), 101–117.

65. Geng, L., Xu, J., Ye, L., Zhou, W., &
Zhou, K. (2015). Connections with na-
ture and environmental behaviors. *PLoS
ONE, 10*(5), e0127247.

66. Klein, S. A., & Hilbig, B. E. (2018). How
virtual nature experiences can promote
pro-environmental behavior. *Journal of
Environmental Psychology, 60,* 41–47.

67. Soliman, M., Peetz, J., & Davydenko, M.
(2017). The impact of immersive technology on nature relatedness and pro-environmental behavior. *Journal of Media
Psychology, 29,* 8–17.

68. Panno, A., Giacomantonio, M., Carrus, G., Maricchiolo, F., Pirchio, S., & Mannetti, L. (2018). Mindfulness, pro-environmental behavior, and belief in climate change: The mediating role of social dominance. *Environment and Behavior*, *50*(8), 864–888.

69. Ray, T. N., Franz, S. A., Jarrett, N. L., & Pickett, S. M. (2020). Nature enhanced meditation: Effects on mindfulness, connectedness to nature, and pro-environmental behavior. *Environment and Behavior*, early online release.

70. Arendt, F., & Matthes, J. (2016). Nature documentaries, connectedness to nature, and pro-environmental behavior. *Environmental Communication*, *10*(4), 453–472. https://doi.org/10.1080/17524032.2014.993415

71. Rosa, C. D., Profice, C. C., & Collado, S. (2018). Nature experiences and adults' self-reported pro-environmental behaviors: The role of connectedness to nature and childhood nature experiences. *Frontiers in Psychology*, *9*, 1055. https://doi.org/10.3389/fpsyg.2018.01055

72. Collado, S., & Corraliza, J. A. (2015). Children's restorative experiences and self-reported environmental behaviors. *Environment and Behavior, 47,* 38–56. https://doi.org/10.1177/0013916513492417

73. Kals, E., Schumacher, D., & Montada, L. (1999). Emotional affinity toward nature as a motivational basis to protect nature. *Environment and Behavior, 31,* 178–202. https://doi.org/10.1177/00139169921972056

74. Lawrence, E. K. (2012). Visitation to natural areas on campus and its relation to place identity and environmentally responsible behaviors. *The Journal of Environmental Education, 43,* 93–106. https://doi.org/10.1080/00958964.2011.604654

75. Larson, L. R., Whiting, J. W., & Green, G. T. (2011). Exploring the influence of outdoor recreation participation on pro-environmental behaviour in a demographically diverse population. *Local Environment, 16,* 67–86. https://doi.org/10.1080/13549839.2010.548373

76. Collado, S., Staats, H., & Corraliza, J. A. (2013). Experiencing nature in children's summer camps: Affective, cognitive and behavioural consequences. *Journal of Environmental Psychology, 33,* 37–44. https://doi.org/10.1016/j.jenvp.2012.08.002

77. Charles, C., & Cajete, G. A. (2020). Wisdom traditions, science and care for the Earth: Pathways to responsible action. *Ecopsychology, 12*(2), 65–70. https://doi.org/10.1089/eco.2020.0020

78. Lefale, P. F. (2010). Ua 'afa le Aso: Stormy weather today: Traditional ecological knowledge of weather and climate. The Samoa experience. *Climatic Change, 100,* 317–355. https://doi.org/10.1007/s10584-009-9722-z

79. King, D. N. T., Skipper, A., & Tawhai, W. B. (2008). Mäori environmental knowledge of local weather and climate change in Aotearoa – New Zealand. *Climatic Change, 90,* 385–409. https://doi.org/10.1007/s10584-007-9372-y

80. Kalanda-Joshua, M., Ngongondo, C., Chipeta, L., & Mpembeka, F. (2011). Integrating indigenous knowledge with conventional science: Enhancing localized climate and weather forecasts in Nessa, Mulanje, Malawi. *Physics and Chemistry of the Earth, Parts A/B/C, 36*, 996–1003. https://doi.org/10.1016/j.pce.2011.08.001

81. Green, D., Billy, J., & Tapim, A. (2010). Indigenous Australians' knowledge of weather and climate. *Climatic Change, 100*(2), 337–354. https://doi.org/10.1007/s10584-010-9803-z

82. Riedlinger, D., & Berkes, F. (2001). Contributions of traditional knowledge to understanding climate change in the Canadian Arctic. *Polar Record, 37*(203), 315–328. https://doi.org/10.1017/S0032247400017058

83. Garay-Barayazarra, G., & Puri, R. K. (2011). Smelling the monsoon: Senses and traditional weather forecasting knowledge among the Kenyah Badeng farmers of Sarawak, Malaysia. *Indian Journal of Traditional Knowledge, 10*(1), 21–30. https://kar.kent.ac.uk/31520/

84. Goebbert, K., Jenkins-Smith, H. C., Klockow, K., Nowlins, M. C., & Silva, C. L. (2012). Weather, climate, and worldviews: The sources and consequences of public perceptions of changes in local weather patterns. *Weather, Climate, and Society, 4*(2), 132–144. https://doi.org/10.1175/WCAS-D-11-00044.1

85. Klockow, K. E., Peppler, R. A., & McPherson, R. A. (2014). Tornado folk science in Alabama and Mississippi in the 27 April 2011 tornado outbreak. *GeoJournal, 79*(6), 791–804. https://doi.org/1007/s10708-013-9518-6

86. Hoekstra, S., Klockow, K., Riley, R., Brotzge, J., Brooks, H., & Erickson, S. (2011). A preliminary look at the social perspective of warn-on-forecast: Preferred tornado warning lead time and the general public's perceptions of weather risks. *Weather, Climate, and Society, 3*(2), 128–140. https://doi.org/10.1175/2011wcas1076.1

87. Allan, J., Ripberger, J. T., Ybarra, V. T., & Cokely, E. T. (2017). Tornado risk literacy: Beliefs, biases, and vulnerability. *Proceedings of the 13th International Conference on Naturalistic Decision Making*, Bath, U.K., 284–290.

88. Sims, J. H., & Baumann, D. D. (1972). The tornado threat: Coping styles of the North and South. *Science, 176*(4042), 1386–1392. https://doi.org/10.1126/science.176.4042.1386

89. Mason, L. R., Ellis, K. N., Winchester, B., & Schexnayder, S. (2018). Tornado warnings at night: Who gets the message? *Weather, Climate, and Society, 10*(3), 561–568. https://doi.org/10.1175/wcas-d-17-0114.1

90. McClure, J., Allen, M. W., & Walkey, F. (2001). Countering fatalism: Causal information in news reports affects judgments about earthquake damage. *Basic and Applied Social Psychology, 23*(2), 109–121. https://doi.org/10.1207/s15324834basp2302_3

91. Cohen, D., & Nisbett, R. E. (1998). Are there differences in fatalism between rural Southerners and Midwesterners? *Journal of Applied Social Psychology, 28*(23), 2181–2195. https://doi.org/10.1111/j.1559-1816.1998.tb01366.x

92. Akesson, J., Ashworth-Hayes, S., Hahn, R., Metcalfe, R. D., & Rasooly, I. (2020). *Fatalism, beliefs, and behaviors during the COVID-19 pandemic.* National Bureau of Economic Research Working Paper #27245. https://doi.org/10.3386/w27245

93. Jimenez, T., Restar, A., Helm, P. J., Cross, R. I., Barath, D., & Arndt, J. (2020). Fatalism in the context of COVID-19: Perceiving coronavirus as a death sentence predicts reluctance to perform recommended preventative behaviors. *SSM – Population Health, 11*, 100615. https://doi.org/10.1016/j.ssmph.2020.100615

94. Nunley, C., & Sherman-Morris, K. (2020). What people know about the weather. *Bulletin of the American Meteorological Society, 101*(7), E1225–E1240. https://doi.org/10.1175/BAMS-D-19-0081.1

95. Walther, J. B. (2017). The merger of mass and interpersonal communication via new media: Integrating metaconstructs. *Human Communication Research, 43*(4), 559–572. https://doi.org/10.1111/hcre.12122

96. Egan, P. J., & Mullin, M. (2012). Turning personal experience into political attitudes: The effect of local weather on Americans' perceptions about global warming. *The Journal of Politics, 74*(3), 796–809. https://doi.org/10.1017/s0022381612000448

97. Li, Y., Johnson, E. J., & Zaval, L. (2011). Local warming: Daily temperature change influences belief in global warming. *Psychological Science, 22*, 454–459. https://doi.org/10.1177/0956797611400913

98. Hamilton, L. C., & Stampone, M. D. (2013). Blowin' in the wind: Short-term weather and belief in anthropomorphic climate change. *Weather, Climate, and Society*, 5, 112–119. https://doi.org/1175/WCAS-D-12-00048.1

99. Schwartz, M. (2010, March 13). *Majority of Americans continue to believe global warming is happening*. Stanford University Woods Institute for the Environment. https://woodsinstitute.stanford.edu/system/files/publications/Krosnick-20090312.pdf

100. Graybill, J. K. (2012). Imagining resilience: Situating perceptions and emotions about climate change on Kamchatka, Russia. *GeoJournal*, *77*(5), https://doi.org/10.1007/s10708-012-9468-4

101. Forbes, B., & Stammler, F. (2009). Arctic climate change discourse: The contrasting politics of research agendas in the West and Russia. *Polar Research*, 28, 28–42.

102. Norgaard, K. M. (2011). *Living in denial: Climate change, emotions and everyday life*. MIT Press.

103. Dai, J., Kesternich, M., Löschel, A., &
Ziegler, A. (2015). Extreme weather experiences and climate change beliefs in
China: An econometric analysis. *Ecological Economics*, *116*, 310–321.
https://doi.org/10.1016/j.ecole-
con.2015.05.001

104. Jamelske, E., Barrett, J., & Boulter, J.
(2013). Comparing climate change awareness, perceptions, and beliefs of college
students in the United States and China.
*Journal of Environmental Studies and Sci-
ences*, *3*(3), 269–278. https://doi.org/
10.1007/s13412-013-0144-x

105. Xue, W., Hine, D. W., Marks, A. D. G.,
Phillips, W. J., and Zhao, S. (2016). Cultural worldviews and climate change: A
view from China. *Asian Journal of Social
Psychology*, *19*(2), 134–144.
https://doi.org/10.1111/ajsp.12116

106. Costello, A., Maslin, M., Montgomery, H., Johnson, A. M., & Ekins, P. (2011). Global health and climate change: Moving from denial and catastrophic fatalism to positive action. *Philosophical Transactions of the Royal Society A: Mathematical, Physical and Engineering Sciences*, *369*(1942), 1866–1882. https://doi.org/10.1098/rsta.2011.0007

107. Mayer, A., & Smith, E. K. (2019). Unstoppable climate change? The influence of fatalistic beliefs about climate change on behavioural change and willingness to pay cross-nationally. *Climate Policy*, *19*(4), 511–523. https://doi.org/10.1080/14693062.2018.1532872

108. Entwistle, T. (2020). Why nudge sometimes fails: Fatalism and the problem of behaviour change. *Policy & Politics*, early online release. https://doi.org/10.1332/030557320X15832072208458

109. Brechin, S. R., & Bhandari, M. (2011). Perceptions of climate change worldwide. *Wiley Interdisciplinary Reviews: Climate Change*, *2*(6), 871–885. https://doi.org/10.1002/wcc.146

110. Lee, T. M., Markowitz, E. M., Howe, P. D., Ko, C.-Y., & Leiserowitz, A. A. (2015). Predictors of public climate change awareness and risk perception around the world. *Nature Climate Change, 5*(11), 1014–1020. https://doi.org/10.1038/nclimate2728

111. Lumbroso, D., Brown, E., & Ranger, N. (2016). Stakeholders' perceptions of the overall effectiveness of early warning systems and risk assessments for weather-related hazards in Africa, the Caribbean and South Asia. *Natural Hazards, 84*(3), 2121–2144. https://doi.org/10.1007/s11069-016-2537-0

112. Dexter, E. G. (1904). *Weather influences: An empirical study of the mental and physiological effects of definite meteorological conditions.* Macmillan.

113. Stewart, A. E. (2015). Edwin Grant Dexter: An early researcher in human behavioral biometeorology. *International Journal of Biometeorology, 59*, 745–758. https://doi.org/10.1007/200484-014-0888-3

114. Ranson, M. (2014). Crime, weather, and climate change. *Journal of Environmental Economics and Management, 67*(3), 274–302. https://doi.org/10.1016/j.jeem.2013.11.008

115. Field, S. (1992). The effect of temperature on crime. *British Journal of Criminology, 32*(3), 340–351.

116. Murataya, R., & Gutiérrez, D. R. (2013). Effects of weather on crime. *International Journal of Humanities and Social Science, 3*(10), 71–75.

117. Butke, P., & Sheridan, S. C. (2010). An analysis of the relationship between weather and aggressive crime in Cleveland, Ohio. *Weather, Climate, and Society, 2*(2), 127–139. https://doi.org/10.1175/2010WCAS1043.1

118. McDowall, D., Loftin, C., & Pate, M. (2012). Seasonal cycles in crime, and their variability. *Journal of Quantitative Criminology, 28*(3), 389–410. https://doi.org/10.1007/s10940-011-9145-7

119. Horrocks, J., & Menclova, A. K. (2011). The effects of weather on crime. *New Zealand Economic Papers*, *45*(3), 231–254. https://doi.org/10.1080/00779954.2011.572544

120. Reifman, A. S., Larrick, R. P., & Fein, S. (1991). Temper and temperature on the diamond: The heat-aggression relationship in Major League Baseball. *Personality and Social Psychology Bulletin*, *17*(5), 580–585. https://doi.org/10.11770146167291175013

121. Rotton, J., & Cohn, E. G. (2000). Weather, disorderly conduct, and assaults: From social contact to social avoidance. *Environment and Behavior*, *32*, 651–673. https://doi.org/10.1177/0013916500325004

122. Deisenhammer, E. A. (2003). Weather and suicide: The present state of knowledge on the association of meteorological factors with suicidal behaviour. *Acta Psychiatrica Scandinavica*, *108*(6), 402–409. https://doi.org/10.1046/j.0001-690x.2003.00209.x

123. Dixon, P. G., & Kalkstein, A. J. (2016). Where are weather-suicide associations valid? An examination of nine US counties with varying seasonality. *International Journal of Biometeorology*, *62*(5), 685–697. https://doi.org/10.1007/s00484-016-1265-1

124. Burke, M., González, F., Baylis, P., Heft-Neal, S., Baysan, C., Basu, S., & Hsiang, S. (2018). Higher temperatures increase suicide rates in the United States and Mexico. *Nature Climate Change*, *8*(8), 723–729. https://doi.org/10.1038/s41558-018-0222-x

125. Gao, J., Cheng, Q., Duan, J., Xu, Z., Bai, L., Zhang, Y., Zhang, H., Wang, S., Zhang, Z., & Su, H. (2019). Ambient temperature, sunlight duration, and suicide: A systematic review and meta-analysis. *Science of The Total Environment*, *646*, 1021–1029. https://doi.org/10.1016/j.scitotenv.2018.07.098

126. Bando, D. H., Teng, C. T., Volpe, F. M., Masi, E. de, Pereira, L. A., & Braga, A. L. (2017). Suicide and meteorological factors in São Paulo, Brazil, 1996-2011: A time series analysis. *Revista Brasileira de Psiquiatria, 39*(3), 220–227. https://doi.org/10.1590/1516-4446-2016-2057

127. Miller, G. A. (2003). The cognitive revolution: A historical perspective. *Trends in Cognitive Sciences, 7*(3), 141–143. https://doi.org/10.1016/S1364-6613(03)00029-9

128. Humble, M. B. (2010). Vitamin D., light and mental health. *Journal of Photochemistry and Photobiology B: Biology, 101*, 142–149. https://doi.org/10.1016/j.jphotobiol.2010.08.003

129. Penckofer, S., Kouba, J., Byrn, M., & Estwing Ferrans, C. (2010). Vitamin D and depression: Where is all the sunshine? *Issues in Mental Health Nursing, 31*(6), 385–393. https://doi.org/10.3109/01612840903437657

130. Carlson, M., Charlin, V., & Miller, N. (1988). Positive mood and helping behavior: A test of six hypotheses. *Journal of Personality and Social Psychology, 55*(2), 211–229.

131. Cunningham, M. R. (1979). Weather, mood, and helping behavior: Quasi experiments with the Sunshine Samaritan. *Journal of Personality and Social Psychology, 37*(11), 1947-1956. https://.doi.org/10.1037/0022-3514.37.11.1947

132. Guéguen, N., & Lamy, L. (2013). Weather and helping: Additional evidence of the effect of the Sunshine Samaritan. *The Journal of Social Psychology, 153*(2), 123–126. https://doi.org/10.1080/00224545.2012.720618

133. Guéguen, N., & Stefan, J. (2013). Hitchhiking and the "Sunshine Driver": Further effects of weather conditions on helping behavior. *Psychological Reports, 113*(3), 994–1000. https://doi.org/10.2466/17.07.pr0.113x30z8

134. Guéguen, N. (2013). Weather and smiling contagion: A quasi experiment with the smiling sunshine. *Journal of Nonverbal Behavior, 37*(1), 51–55. https://doi.org/10.1007/s10919-012-0140-y

135. Sanders, J., & Brizzolara, M. S. (1982). Relationships between weather and mood. *Journal of General Psychology, 107,* 155–156.

136. Parrot, G., & Sabini, J. (1990). Mood and memory under natural conditions: Evidence for mood incongruent recall. *Journal of Personality and Social Psychology, 59,* 321–336.

137. Schwarz, N., & Clore, G. L. (1983). Mood, misattribution, and judgements of well-being: Informative and directive functions of affective states. *Journal of Personality and Social Psychology, 45*(3), 513–523.

138. Messner, C., & Wänke, M. (2011). Good weather for Schwarz and Clore. *Emotion, 11*(2), 436–437. https://doi.org/10.1037/a0022821

139. Goldstein, K. M. (1972). Weather, mood, and internal-external control. *Perceptual Motor Skills, 35*, 786.

140. Howarth, E., & Hoffman, M. S. (1984). A multidimensional approach to the relationship between mood and weather. *British Journal of Psychology, 75*, 15–23.

141. Keller, M. C., Fredrickson, B. L., Ybarra, O., Côté, S., Johnson, K., Mikels, J., Conway, A., & Wager, T. (2005). A warm heart and a clear head: The contingent effects of weather on mood and cognition. *Psychological Science, 16*(9), 724–731. https://doi.org/10.1111/j.1467-9280.2005.01602.x

142. Denissen, J. A., Butalid, L., Penke, L., & van Aken, M. A. G. (2008). The effects of weather on daily mood: A multilevel approach. *Emotion, 8*(5), 662–667. https://doi.org/10.1037/a0013497

143. Klimstra, T. A., Frijns, T., Keijsers, L.,
Denissen, J. J. A., Raaijmakers, Q. A. W.,
van Aken, M. A. G., Koot, H. M., van
Lier, P. A. C., & Meeus, W. H. J. (2011).
Come rain or come shine: Individual dif-
ferences in how weather affects mood.
Emotion, 11(6), 1495–1499.
https://doi.org/10.1037/a0024649

144. Hannak, A., Anderson, E., Feldman Bar-
ret, L., Lehmann S., Mislove, A., & Riede-
wald, M. (2012). Tweetin' in the rain:
Exploring societal-scale effects of weather
on mood. *Proceedings of the Sixth International AAAI Conference on Weblogs and
Social Media*, 479–482.
https://www.aaai.org/ocs/index.php/
ICWSM/ICWSM12/paper/viewFile/
4648/5036

145. Baylis, P., Obradovich, N., Kryvasheyeu,
Y., Chen, H., Coviello, L., Moro, E., Ce-
brian, M., & Fowler, J. H. (2018).
Weather impacts expressed sentiment.
PLoS ONE, 13(4), e0195750.
https://doi.org/10.1371/jour-
nal.pone.0195750

146. Kööts, L., Realo, A., & Allik, J. (2011). The influence of the weather on affective experience. *Journal of Individual Differences, 32*(2), 74–84. https://doi.org/10.1027/1614-0001/a000037

147. Lucas, R. E., & Lawless, N. M. (2013). Does life seem better on a sunny day? Examining the association between daily weather conditions and life satisfaction judgements. *Journal of Personality and Social Psychology, 104*(5), 872–884. https://doi.org/10.1037/a0032124

148. Yap, S. C. Y., Wortman, J., Anusic, I., Baker, S. G., Scherer, L. D., Donnellan, M. B., & Lucas, R. E. (2017). The effect of mood on judgments of subjective well-being: Nine tests of the judgment model. *Journal of Personality and Social Psychology, 113*(6), 939–961. https://doi.org/10.1037/pspp0000115

149. Gleick, J. (2008). *Chaos: Making a new science*. Penguin Books.

150. Stewart, A. E., & Blau, J. J. C. (2019). Weather as ecological events. *Ecological Psychology, 31*(2), 107–126. https://doi.org/10.1080/10407413.2018.1552496

151. Stewart, A. E., & Oh, J. (2019). Weather and climate as events: Contributions to the public idea of climate change. *International Journal of Big Data Mining for Global Warming*, *1*(2). https://doi.org/10.1142/S2630534819500050

152. Stewart, A. E., & Bolton, M. J. (2021). Analogue weather in a digital world: On the value of integrating both the physical and the technological in day-to-day experiences of weather. *PsyArxiv*, preprint. https://doi.org/10.31234/osf.io/5yrg9

153. Carlson, N. R., & Birkett, M. A. (2017). *Physiology of behavior* (12th edition, global edition). Pearson.

154. White, P. R. (2011). A phenomenological self-inquiry into ecological consciousness. *Ecopsychology*, *3*(1), 41–50. https://doi.org/10.1089/eco.2010.0054

155. Schweitzer, R. D., Glab, H., & Brymer, E. (2018). The human-nature experience: A phenomenological-psychoanalytic perspective. *Frontiers in Psychology*, *9*, 969. https://doi.org/10.3389/fpsyg.2018.00969

156. Naor, L., & Mayseless, O. (2020). How personal transformation occurs following a single peak experience in nature: A phenomenological account. *Journal of Humanistic Psychology, 60*(6), 865–888. https://doi.org/ 10.11770022167817714692

157. Kemkes, R. J., & Akerman, S. (2019). Contending with the nature of climate change: Phenomenological interpretations from northern Wisconsin. *Emotion, Space, and Society, 33*, 100614. https://doi.org/10.1016/j.emospa.2019.100614

158. Schauer, B., Kock, K., Lemieux, L., & Willey, K. (2016). *How immersion in nature impacts the human spirit: A phenomenological study*. Unpublished Master's thesis, St. Catharine University. https://sophia.stkate.edu/cgi/viewcontent.cgi?article=1007&context=ma_hhs

159. Gray, E. K., & Watson, D. (2007). Assessing positive and negative affect via self-report. In J. A. Coan, & J. J. B. Allen, (Eds.), *Handbook of emotion elicitation and assessment* (pp. 171–183). Oxford University Press.

160. Rosenman, R., Tennekoon, V., & Hill, L. G. (2011). Measuring bias in self-reported data. *International Journal of Behavioural and Health Care Research*, *2*(4), 320–332. https://doi.org/10.1504/IJBHR.2011.043414

161. Rosenthal, N. E., Sack, D. A., & Gillin, J. C. (1984). Seasonal affective disorder: A description of the syndrome and preliminary findings with light therapy. *Archives of General Psychiatry*, *41*(1), 72–80. https://doi.org/10.1001/archpsyc.1984.01790120076010

162. Ho, K. W. D., Han, S., Nielsen, J. V., Jancic, D., Hing, B., Fiedorowicz, J., Weissman, M. M., Levinson, D. F., & Potash, J. B. (2018). Genome-wide association study of seasonal affective disorder. *Translational Psychiatry*, *8*(1), 190. https://doi.org/10.1038/s41398-018-0246-z

163. Mersch, P. P. A., Middendorp, H. M., Bouhuys, A. L., Beersma, D. G. M., & van den Hoofdakker, R. H. (1999). Seasonal affective disorder and latitude: A review of the literature. *Journal of Affective Disorders*, *53*(1), 35–48. https://doi.org/10.1016/s0165-0327(98)00097-4

164. Rosen, L. N., Targum, S. D., Terman, M., Bryant, M. J., Hoffman, H., Kasper, S. F., Hamovit, J. R., Docherty, J. P., Welch, B., & Rosenthal, N. E. (1990). Prevalence of seasonal affective disorder at four latitudes. *Psychiatry Research*, *31*, 131–144. https://doi.org/10.1016/0165-1781(90)90116-M

165. Pjrek, E., Baldinger-Melich, P., Spies, M., Papageorgiou, K., Kasper, S., & Winkler, D. (2016). Epidemiology and socioeconomic impact of seasonal affective disorder in Austria. *European Psychiatry*, *32*, 28–33. https://doi.org/10.1016/j.eurpsy.2015.11.001

166. Morales-Muñoz, I., Koskinen, S., & Partonen, T. (2017). Differences in clinical and cognitive variables in seasonal affective disorder compared to depressive-related disorders: Evidence from a population-based study in Finland. *European Psychiatry*, *44*, 9–16. https://doi.org/10.1016/j.eurpsy.2017.03.003

167. Kurata, Y., Izawa, S., & Nomura, S. (2016). Seasonality in mood and behaviours of Japanese residents in high-latitude regions: Transnational cross-sectional study. *BioPsychoSocial Medicine*, *10*(1). https://doi.org/10.1186/s13030-016-0084-2

168. Patten, S. B., Williams, J. V. A., Lavorato, D. H., Bulloch, A. G. M., Fiest, K. M., Wang, J. L., & Sajobi, T. T. (2016). Seasonal variation in major depressive episode prevalence in Canada. *Epidemiology and Psychiatric Sciences*, *26*(2), 169–176. https://doi.org/10.1017/s2045796015001183

169. Patten, S. B., Williams, J. V. A., Lavorato, D. H., Wang, J. L., & Bulloch, A. G. M. (2016). Major depression prevalence increases with latitude in Canada. *The Canadian Journal of Psychiatry*, *62*(1), 62–66. https://doi.org/10.1177/0706743716673323

170. Sandman, N., Merikanto, I., Määttänen, H., Valli, K., Kronholm, E., Laatikainen, T., Partonen, T., & Paunio, T. (2016). Winter is coming: Nightmares and sleep problems during seasonal affective disorder. *Journal of Sleep Research*, *25*(5), 612–619. https://doi.org/10.1111/jsr.12416

171. Basnet, S., Merikanto, I., Lahti, T., Männistö, S., Laatikainen, T., Vartiainen, E., & Partonen, T. (2016). Seasonal variations in mood and behavior associate with common chronic diseases and symptoms in a population-based study. *Psychiatry Research*, *238*, 181–188. https://doi.org/10.1016/j.psychres.2016.02.023

172. Stewart, A. E., Roecklein, K. A., Tanner, S., & Kimlin, M. G. (2014). Possible contributions of skin pigmentation and vitamin D in a polyfactorial model of seasonal affective disorder. *Medical Hypotheses*, *83*(5), 517–525. https://doi.org/10.1016/j.mehy.2014.09.010

173. Kerr, D. C. R., Zava, D. T., Piper, W. T., Saturn, S. R., Frei, B., & Gombart, A. F. (2015). Associations between vitamin D levels and depressive symptoms in healthy young adult women. *Psychiatry Research*, *227*(1), 46–51. https://doi.org/10.1016/j.psychres.2015.02.016

174. Anglin, R. E. S., Samaan, Z., Walter, S. D., & McDonald, S. D. (2013). Vitamin D deficiency and depression in adults: Systematic review and meta-analysis. British *Journal of Psychiatry*, *202*(2), 100–107. https://doi.org/10.1192/bjp.bp.111.106666

175. Webb, A. R., Kline, L., & Holick, M. F. (1988). Influence of season and latitude on the cutaneous synthesis of vitamin D3: Exposure to winter sunlight in Boston and Edmonton will not promote vitamin D3 synthesis in human skin. *The Journal of Clinical Endocrinology & Metabolism*, *67*(2), 373–378. https://doi.org/10.1210/jcem-67-2-373

176. Webb, A. R., DeCosta, B. R., & Holick, M. F. (1989). Sunlight regulates the cutaneous production of vitamin D3 by causing its photodegradation. *The Journal of Clinical Endocrinology & Metabolism*, *68*(5), 882–887. https://doi.org/10.1210/jcem-68-5-882

177. Engelsen, O., Brustad, M., Aksnes, L., & Lund, E. (2005). Daily duration of vitamin D synthesis in human skin with relation to latitude, total ozone, altitude, ground cover, aerosols and cloud thickness. *Photochemistry and Photobiology*, *81*(6), 1287. https://doi.org/10.1562/2004-11-19-rn-375

178. Rohan, K. J., Tierney Lindsey, K., Roeklein, K. A., & Lacy, T. J. (2004). Cognitive-behavioral therapy, light therapy, and their combination in treating seasonal affective disorder. *Journal of Affective Science*, *80*, 273–283. https://doi.org/10.1016/S0165-0327(03)00098-3

179. Rohan, K. J., Roecklein, K. A., Tierney Lindsey, K., Johnson, L. G., Lippy, R. D., Lacy, T. J., & Barton, F. B. (2007). A randomized controlled trial of cognitive-behavioral therapy, light therapy, and their combination for seasonal affective disorder. *Journal of Consulting and Clinical Psychology, 75*(3), 489–500. https://doi.org/10.1037/0022-006X.75.3.489

180. Rohan, K. J., Mahon, J. N., Evans, M., Ho, S.-Y., Meyerhoff, J., Postolache, T. T., & Vacek, P. M. (2015). Randomized trial of cognitive-behavioral therapy versus light therapy for seasonal affective disorder: Acute outcomes. *American Journal of Psychiatry, 172*(9), 862–869. https://doi.org/10.1176/appi.ajp.2015.14101293

181. Morales-Muñoz, I., Koskinen, S., & Partonen, T. (2017). Seasonal affective disorder and alcohol abuse disorder in a population-based study. *Psychiatry Research, 253*, 91–98. https://doi.org/10.1016/j.psychres.2017.03.029

182. Ventura-Cots, M., Watts, A. E., Cruz-Lemini, M., Shah, N. D., Ndugga, N., McCann, P., Barritt, A. S., IV., Jain, A., Ravi, S., Fernandez-Carrillo, C., Abraldes, J. G., Altamirano, J., & Bataller, R. (2019). Colder weather and fewer sunlight hours increase alcohol consumption and alcoholic cirrhosis worldwide. *Hepatology, 69*(5), 1916–1930. https://doi.org/10.1002/hep.30315

183. Østergaard Madsen, H., Dam, H., & Hageman, I. (2016). High prevalence of seasonal affective disorder among persons with severe visual impairment. *British Journal of Psychiatry, 208*(1), 56–61. https://doi.org/10.1192/bjp.bp.114.162354

184. Kurczab, B., Ćwiek, A., Kramarczyk, K., Witkowska, A., Drzyzga, K., & Kucia, K. (2019). The prevalence of seasonal affective disorder among the blind and patients with serious visual impairment. *Psychiatria Danubina, 31*, 579–584.

185. Schmidt, T. M., & Kofuji, P. (2008). Novel insights into non-image forming visual processing in the retina. *Cellscience, 5*(1), 77–83.

186. Coleman, J. S. M., Newby, K. D., Multon, K. D., & Taylor, C. (2014). Weathering the storm: Revisiting severe-weather phobia. *Bulletin of the American Meteorological Society, 95*(8), 1179–1183. https://doi.org/10.1175/bams-d-13-00137.1

187. Greening, L., & Dollinger, S. J. (1992). Adolescents' perceptions of lightning and tornado risks. *Journal of Applied Social Psychology, 22*, 755–762.

188. Lonigan, C. S., Shannon, M. P., Taylor, C. M., & Finch, A. J. (1994). Children exposed to disaster. II: Risk factors for the development of post-traumatic symptomatology. *Journal of the American Academy of Child and Adolescent Psychiatry, 33*, 94–105.

189. Nelson, A.L., Vorstenbosch, V. & Antony, M.M. (2014). Assessing fear of storms and severe weather: Validation of the Storm Fear Questionnaire (SFQ). *Journal of Psychopathology and Behavioral Assessment, 36*, 105. https://doi.org/10.1007/s10862-013-9370-5

190. Watt, M. C., & DiFrancescantonio, S. L. (2012). Who's afraid of the big bad wind? Origins of severe weather phobia. *Journal of Psychopathological Behavior Assessment, 34*, 440–450. https://doi.org/10.1007/s10862-012-9308-3

191. Westefeld, J. S. (1996). Severe weather phobia: An exploratory study. *Journal of Clinical Psychology, 52*, 509–515.

192. Westefeld, J. S., Less, A., Ansley, T., & Yi, H. S. (2006). Severe-weather phobia. *Bulletin of the American Meteorological Society*, *87*(6), 747–750. https://doi.org/10.1175/BAMS-87-6-747

193. Dreschel, N. A. (2010). The effects of fear and anxiety on health and lifespan in pet dogs. *Applied Animal Behaviour Science*, *125*(3-4), 157–162. https://doi.org/10.1016/j.applanim.2010.04.003

194. Rim, Y. (1975). Psychological test performance during climatic heat stress from dessert winds. *International Journal of Biometeorology*, *19*(1), 37–40.

195. Strauss, S. (2007). An ill wind: The Foehn in Leukerbad and beyond. *Journal of the Royal Anthropological Institute*, *13*(1), 5165–5181. https://doi.org/10.1111/j.1467-9655.2007.00406.x

196. Cooke, L. J., Rose, M. S., & Becker, W. J. (2000). Chinook winds and migraine headache. *Neurology*, *54*(2), 302–302. https://doi.org/10.1212/wnl.54.2.302

197. Wandersman, A. H., & Hallman, W. K. (1993). Are people acting irrationally? Understanding public concerns about environmental threats. *American Psychologist, 48*, 681–686. https://doi.org/10.1037/0003-066X.48.6.681

198. McMichael, A. J., Haines, A., Sloof, R., & Kovats, S. (1996). *Climate change and human health*. World Health Organization. https://apps.who.int/iris/bitstream/handle/10665/62989/WHO_EHG_96.7.pdf

199. Ingle, H., & Mikulewicz, M. (2005). Mental health and climate change: Tackling invisible injustice. *The Lancet Planetary Health, 4*(4), e128–e130. https://doi.org/10.1016/S2542-5196(20)30081-4

200. Albrecht, G., Sartore, G.-M., Connor, L., Higginbotham, N., Freeman, S., Kelly, B., Stain, H., Tonna, A., & Pollard, G. (2007). Solastalgia: The distress caused by environmental change. *Australasian Psychiatry, 15*(1), 595–598. https://doi.org/10.1080/10398560701701288

201. Morrissey, S. A., & Reser, J. P. (2007).
Natural disasters, climate change and
mental health considerations for rural
Australia. *Australian Journal of Rural
Health*, *15*(2), 120–125. https://doi.org/
10.1111/j.1440-1584.2007.00865.x

202. Fritze, J., Blashki, G. A., Burke, S., &
Wiseman, J. (2008). Hope, despair, and
transformation: Climate change and the
promotion of mental health and wellbeing. *International Journal of Mental
Health Systems*, *2*, 13. https://doi.org/
10.1186/1752-4458-2-13

203. Randall, R. (2009). Loss and climate
change: The cost of parallel narratives.
Ecopsychology, *1*, 118–129.
https://doi.org/10.1089/eco.2009.0034

204. Berry, H. L., Bowen, K., & Kjellstrom, T.
(2010). Climate change and mental
health: A causal pathways framework. *International Journal of Public Health*, *55*,
123–132. https://doi.org/10.1007/
s00038-009-0112-0

205. Berry, H. L., Hogan, A., Owen, J., Rickwood, D., & Fragar, L. (2011). Climate change and farmers' mental health: Risks and responses. *Asia Pacific Journal of Public Health*, *23*(2), 119S–132S. https://doi.org/10.1177/1010539510392556

206. Stewart, A. E. (2021). Psychometric properties of the Climate Change Worry Scale. *International Journal of Research in Public Health*, *18*(2), 494. https://doi.org/10.3390/ijerph18020494

207. Bourque, F., Cunsolo Wilcox, A. (2014). Climate change: The next challenge for public mental health? *International Review of Psychiatry*, *26*(4), 415–422. https://doi.org/10.3109/09540261.2014.925851

208. Cianconi, P., Betrò, S., & Janiri, L. (2020). The impact of climate change on mental health: A systematic descriptive review. *Frontiers in Psychology*, *11*, 74. https://doi.org/3389/fpsyt.2020.00074

209. Clayton, S. (2020). Climate anxiety: Psychological responses to climate change. *Journal of Anxiety Disorders*, *74*, 102263. https://doi.org/10.1016/j.janxdis.2020.102263

210. Clayton, S., & Karazsia, B. T. (2020). Development and validation of a measure of climate change anxiety. *Journal of Environmental Psychology*, *69*, 101434. https://doi.org/10.1016/j.jenvp.2020.101434

211. Doherty, T. J., & Clayton, S. (2011). The psychological impacts of global climate change. *American Psychologist*, *66*(4), 265–276. https://doi.org/10.1037/a0023141

212. Searle, K., & Gow, K. (2010). Do concerns about climate change lead to distress? *International Journal of Climate Change Strategies and Management*, *2*(4), 362–379. https://doi.org/10.1108/17568691011089891

213. Stokols, D., Misra, S., Runnerstrom, M. G., & Hipp, J. A. (2009). Psychology in an age of ecological crisis: From personal angst to collective action. *American Psychologist, 64*, 181–193. https://doi.org/10.1037/a0014717

214. Christensen, J. (2019, May 7). *Climate anxiety is real, but there's something you can do about it*. CNN. https://www.cnn.com/2019/05/07/health/climate-anxiety-eprise/index.html

215. Taylor, M., & Murray, J. (2020, February 10). *'Overwhelming and terrifying': The rise of climate anxiety*. The Guardian. https://www.theguardian.com/environment/2020/feb/10/overwhelming-and-terrifying-impact-of-climate-crisis-on-mental-health

216. Ro, C. (2019, October 10). *The harm from worrying about climate change*. BBC News. https://www.bbc.com/future/article/20191010-how-to-beat-anxiety-about-climate-change-and-eco-awareness

217. Klivans, L. (2020, April 22*). It's hard to think about climate change during a pandemic. Here's how to stay engaged.* National Public Radio. https://www.npr.org/sections/health-shots/2020/04/22/808853706/this-earth-day-is-like-no-other-heres-how-to-grieve-and-stay-engaged

218. Pihkala, P. (2020, April 2). *Climate grief: How we mourn a changing planet.* BBC News. https://www.bbc.com/future/article/20200402-climate-grief-mourning-loss-due-to-climate-change

219. Bolton, M. J., & DePodwin, R. A. (2019). "So what if I'm not OK?" A discussion on meteorologists' emotional wellbeing and healthy coping mechanisms for weather professionals in the face of mental health challenges. *PsyArxiv*, preprint. https://doi.org/10.31234/osf.io/zh2va

220. Bolton, M. J., Stewart, A. E, & Mogil. H. M. (2020). An integrationist, meteorologist-oriented perspective on trauma and mental health coping. *PsyArxiv*, preprint. https://doi.org/10.31234/osf.io/wfntj

221. Bolton, M. J., Mogil, H. M., & Stewart, A. E. (2020). An interdisciplinary perspective on meteorological learning for humanistic psychotherapists facing Earth's changing climate and everyday weather. *The Person-Centered Journal*, *25*(1–2), 152–171. https://adpca.org/article/pcj25/psychotherapist-weather-learning-matthew-j-bolton-h/

222. Mileti, D. S., & Sorensen, J. H. (1990). *Communication of emergency public warnings: A social science perspective and state-of-the-art assessment*. U.S. Department of Energy, Office of Scientific and Technical Information. https://doi.org/2172/6137387

223. Eastern Research Group. (2018). *National Weather Service hazard simplification: Public survey*. https://www.weather.gov/media/hazard-simplification/HazSimp%20Public%20Survey%20-%20Final%20Report%20-%2006-01-18.pdf

224. Sherman-Morris, K. (2013). The public response to hazardous weather events: 25 years of research. *Geography Compass*, *7*(10), 669–685. https://doi.org/10.1111/gec3.12076

225. Lindell, M. K., & Perry, R. W. (2012). The Protective Action Decision Model: Theoretical modifications and additional evidence. *Risk Analysis*, *32*, 616–632. https://doi.org/10.1111/j.1539-6924.2011.01647.x

226. Brotzge, J., & Donner, W. (2013). The tornado warning process: A review of current research, challenges, and opportunities. *Bulletin of the American Meteorological Society*, *94*, 1715–1733. https://doi.org/10.1175/BAMS-D-12-00147.1

227. Mileti, D. S. & O'Brien, P. W. (1992). Warnings during disaster: Normalizing communicated risk. *Social Problems* *39*(1), 40–56. https://doi.org/10.2307/3096912

228. Mileti, D. S. & Darlington, J. D. (1997). The role of searching in shaping reactions to earthquake risk information. *Social Problems*, *44*(1), 89–101. https://doi.org/10.2307/3096875

229. Spence, P. R., Lachlan, K. A. & Griffin, D. R. (2007). Crisis communication, race, and natural disasters. *Journal of Black Studies*, *37*(4), 539–554. https://doi.org/10.11770021934706296192

230. Chaney, P. L. & Weaver, G. S. (2010). The vulnerability of mobile home residents in tornado disasters: the 2008 Super Tuesday Tornado in Macon County, TN. *Weather, Climate and Society*, *2*(3), 190–199. https://doi.org/10.1175/2010WCAS1042.1

231. Hammer, B. & Schmidlin, T. W. (2002). Response to warnings during the May 1999 Oklahoma City tornado: reasons and relative injury rates. *Weather and Forecasting*, *17*(3), 577–581. https://doi.org/10.1175/1520-0434(2002)017<0577:RTWDTM>2.0.CO;2

232. Comstock R. D. & Mallonee, S. (2005). Comparing results to two severe tornadoes in one Oklahoma community. *Disasters, 29*(3), 277–287. https://doi.org/10.1111/j.0361-3666.2005.00291.x

233. Paul, B. K., Brock, V. T., Csiki, S. & Emerson, L. (2003). *Public response to tornado warnings: a comparative study of the May 4 2003 tornados in Kansas, Missouri and Tennessee.* Quick Response #165. Natural Hazards Research Applications and Information Center. https://hazards.colorado.edu/uploads/basicpage/qr165.pdf

234. Sherman-Morris, K. (2010). Tornado warning dissemination and response at a university campus. *Natural Hazards, 52,* 623–638. https://doi.org/10.1007/s11069-009-9405-0

235. Tiefenbacher, J. P., Monfredo, W., Shuey, M. & Cecora, R. J. (2002). *Examining a "near-miss" experience: Awareness, behavior, and post-disaster response among residents on the periphery of a tornado-damage path.* Quick Response Research Report #137. Natural Hazards Research and Applications Information Center. https://hazards.colorado.edu/uploads/basicpage/QR%20137.pdf

236. Thieken, A. H., Kreibich, H., Müller, M. & Merz, B. (2007). Coping with floods: Preparedness, response and recovery of flood-affected residents in Germany in 2002. *Hydrological Sciences Journal, 52*(5), 1016–1037. https://doi.org/10.1623/hysj.52.5.1016

237. Ashley, W. S., Krmenec, A. J., & Schwantes, R. (2008). Vulnerability due to nocturnal tornadoes. *Weather and Forecasting, 23*(5), 795–807. https://doi.org/10.1175/2008waf2222132.1

238. Simmons, K. M., & Sutter, D. (2009). False alarms, tornado warnings, and tornado casualties. *Weather, Climate, and Society*, *1*(1), 38–53. https://doi.org/10.1175/2009WCAS1005.1

239. Ashley, W. S. (2007). Spatial and temporal analysis of tornado fatalities in the United States: 1880–2005. *Weather and Forecasting*, *22*(6), 1214–1228. https://doi.org/10.1175/2007waf2007004.1

240. Ellis, K., Mason, L. R., & Hurley, K. (2020). In the dark: Public perceptions of and National Weather Service forecaster considerations for nocturnal tornadoes in Tennessee. *Bulletin of the American Meteorological Society*, *101*(10), E1677–E1684. https://doi.og/10.1175/bams-d-19-0245.1

241. Fricker, T., & Elsner, J. B. (2020). Unusually devastating tornadoes in the United States: 1995–2016. *Annals of the American Association of Geographers*, *110*(3), 724–738. https://doi.org/10.1080/24694452.2019.1638753

242. Fricker, T. (2020). Tornado-level estimates of socioeconomic and demographic variables. *Natural Hazards Review*, *21*(3), 04020018. https://doi.org/10.1061/(ASCE)NH.1527-6996.0000379

243. Ash, K. D., Egnoto, M. J., Strader, S. M., Ashley, W. S., Roueche, D. B., Klockow-McClain, K. E., Caplen, D., & Dickerson, M. (2020). Structural forces: Perception and vulnerability factors for tornado sheltering within mobile and manufactured housing in Alabama and Mississippi. *Weather, Climate, and Society*, *12*(3), 453–472. https://doi.org/10.1175/WCAS-D-19-0088.1

244. Donner, W., & Rodríguez, H. (2008). Population composition, migration and inequality: The influence of demographic changes on disaster risk and vulnerability. *Social Forces*, *87*(2), 1089–1114. https://doi.org/10.1353/sof.0.0141

245. Donner, W. R., Rodríguez, H., & Diaz, W. (2004). Tornado warnings in three southern states: A qualitative analysis of public response patterns. *Journal of Homeland Security*, *9*(2). https://doi.org/10.1515/1547-7355.1955

246. Lim, J., Loveridge, S., Shupp, R., & Skidmore, M. (2017). Double danger in the double wide: Dimensions of poverty, housing quality and tornado impacts. *Regional Science and Urban Economics, 65*, 1–15. https://doi.org/10.1016/j.regsciurbeco.2017.04.003

247. Dickey, J. E. (2020). *Evaluating various socio-economic factors and their effect on tornado knowledge in Mississippi and Alabama*. Unpublished Master's thesis, Mississippi State University. https://ir.library.msstate.edu/bitstream/handle/11668/20861/Jacob%20Dickey%20-%20Thesis%20Approved%20by%20ETD.pdf?sequence=1

248. Wuepper, D., & Lybbert, T. J. (2017). Perceived self-efficacy, poverty, and economic development. *Annual Review of Resource Economics, 9*, 383–404. https://doi.org/10.1146/annurev-resource-100516-053709

249. Mickelson, K. D., & Williams, S. L. (2008). Perceived stigma of poverty and depression: Examination of interpersonal and intrapersonal mediators. *Journal of Social and Clinical Psychology*, *27*(9), 903–930. https://doi.org/10.1521/jscp.2008.27.9.903

250. Reutter, L. I., Stewart, M. J., Veenstra, G., Love, R., Raphael, D., & Makwarimba, E. (2009). "Who do they think we are, anyway?": Perceptions of and responses to poverty stigma. *Qualitative Health Research*, *19*(3), 297–311. https://doi.org/10.11771049732308330246

251. Silver, A. (2015). Watch or warning? Perceptions, preferences, and usage of forecast information by members of the Canadian public. *Meteorological Applications*, *22*(2), 248–255. https://doi.org/10.1002/met.1452

252. Ripberger, J. T., Silva, C. L., Jenkins-Smith, H. C., Allan, J., Krocak, M., Wehde, W., & Ernst, S. (2020). Exploring community differences in tornado warning reception, comprehension, and response across the United States. *Bulletin of the American Meteorological Society*, *101*(6), E936–E948. https://doi.org/10.1175/BAMS-D-19-0064.1

253. Nagele, D., & Trainor, J. E. (2012). Geographic specificity, tornadoes, and protective action. *Weather, Climate, and Society*, *4*(2), 145–155. https://doi.org/10.1175/WCAS-D-11-00047.1

254. Durage, S. W., Kattan, L., Wirasinghe, S. C., & Ruwanpura, J. Y. (2014). Evacuation behaviour of households and drivers during a tornado. *Natural Hazards*, *71*, 1495–1517. https://doi.org/10.1007/s11069-013-0958-6

255. Ripberger, J. T., Silva, C. L., Jenkins-Smith, H. C., Carlson, D. E., James, M., & Herron, K. G. (2015). False alarms and missed events: The impact and origins of perceived inaccuracy in tornado warning systems. *Risk Analysis*, *35*, 44–56. https://doi.org/10.1111/risa.12262

256. Burke, S., Bethel, J. W., & Britt, A. F. (2012). Assessing disaster preparedness among Latino migrant and seasonal farmworkers in eastern North Carolina. *International Journal of Environmental Research and Public Health*, *9*, 3115–3133. https://doi.org/10.3390/ijerph9093115

257. Zabini, F. (2016). Mobile weather apps or the illusion of certainty. *Meteorological Applications*, *4*, 663-670. https://doi.org/10.1002/met.1589

258. Heilig, R. (2010). How an iPhone can change the weather. In *Proceedings of the 26th Conference on Interactive Information and Processing Systems (IIPS) for Meteorology, Oceanography, and Hydrology*, 17–21 January 2010. American Meteorological Society. https://ams.confex.com/ams/pdfpapers/159723.pdf

259. Phan, M. D., Montz, B. E., Curtis, S., & Rickenbach, T. M. (2018). Weather on the go: An assessment of smartphone mobile weather application use among college students. *Bulletin of the American Meteorological Society, 99*(11), 2245–2257. https://doi.org/10.1175/BAMS-D-18-0020.1

260. Silva, C., Ripberger, J., Jenkins-Smith, H., & Krocak, M. (2017). *Establishing a baseline: Public reception, understanding, and responses to severe weather forecasts and warnings in the contiguous United States.* University of Oklahoma Center for Risk and Crisis Management Reference Report. http://risk.ou.edu/downloads/news/WX17-Reference-Report.pdf

261. Silva, C., Ripberger, J., Jenkins-Smith, H., Krocak, M., & Wehde, W. (2018). *Refining the baseline: Public reception, understanding, and responses to severe weather forecasts and warnings in the contiguous United States.* University of Oklahoma Center for Risk and Crisis Management Reference Report. http://risk.ou.edu/downloads/news/WX18-Reference-Report.pdf

262. Silva, C., Ripberger, J., Jenkins-Smith, H., Krocak, M., Ernst, S., & Bell, A. (2019). *Continuing the baseline: Public reception, understanding, and responses to severe weather forecasts and warnings in the contiguous United States.* University of Oklahoma Center for Risk and Crisis Management Reference Report. http://risk.ou.edu/downloads/news/WX19-Reference-Report.pdf

263. Ripberger, Krocak, M. J., Wehde, W. W., Allan, J. N., Silva, C., & Jenkins-Smith, H. (2019). Measuring tornado warning reception, comprehension, and response in the United States. *Weather, Climate, and Society, 11*(4), 863–880. https://doi.org/10.1175/WCAS-D-19-0015.1

264. Grounds, M. A., & Joslyn, S. L. (2018). Communicating weather forecast uncertainty: Do individual differences matter? *Journal of Experimental Psychology: Applied, 24*(1), 18–33. https://doi.org/10.1037/xap0000165

265. Joslyn, S. L., & Grounds, M. A. (2015). The use of uncertainty forecasts in complex decision tasks and various weather conditions. *Journal of Experimental Psychology: Applied, 21,* 407–417. https://doi.org/10 .1037/xap0000064

266. Joslyn, S. L., & LeClerc, J. E. (2012). Uncertainty forecasts improve weather-related decisions and attenuate the effects of forecast error. *Journal of Experimental Psychology: Applied, 18,* 126–40. https://doi.org/10.1037/a0025185

267. Joslyn, S., & LeClerc, J. (2013). Decisions with uncertainty: The glass half full. *Current Directions in Psychological Science, 22,* 308–315. https://doi.org/10.1177/0963721413481473

268. Roulston, M. S., Bolton, G. E., Kleit, A. N., & Sears-Collins, A. L. (2006). A laboratory study of the benefits of including uncertainty information in weather forecasts. *Weather and Forecasting, 21,* 116–122. https://doi.org/10.1175/WAF887.1

269. Wallsten, T. S., & Budescu, D. V. (1995). A review of human linguistic probability processing: General principles and empirical evidence. *Knowledge Engineering Review, 10*(1), 43–62. https://doi.org/10.1017/S0269888900007256

270. Budescu, D. V., Por, H. H., & Broomell, S. B. (2012). Effective communication of uncertainty in the IPCC reports. *Climatic Change, 113*, 181–200. https://doi.org/10.1007/s10584-011-0330-3

271. Clarke, V. A., Ruffin, C. L., Hill, D. J., & Beamen, A. L. (1992). Ratings of orally presented verbal expressions of probability by a heterogeneous sample. *Journal of Applied Social Psychology, 22*, 638–656. https://doi.org/10.1111/j.1559-1816.1992.tb00995.x

272. Beyth-Marom, R. (1982). How probable is probable? A numerical translation of verbal probability expressions. *Journal of Forecasting, 1*(3), 257–269. https://doi.org/10.1002/for.3980010305

273. Nakao, M. A., & Axelrod, S. (1983).
Numbers are better than words: Verbal
specifications of frequency have no place
in medicine. *The American Journal of
Medicine, 74*(6), 1061–1065.
https://doi.org/10.1016/
0002-9343(83)90819-7

274. Brun, W., & Teigen, K. H. (1988). Verbal
probabilities: Ambiguous, context-depen-
dent, or both? *Organizational Behavior
and Human Decision Processes, 41*(3),
390–404. https://doi.org/10.1016/
0749-5978(88)90036-2

275. Wintle, B. C., Fraser, H., Wills, B. C.,
Nicholson, A. E., & Fidler, F. (2019). Verbal probabilities: Very likely to be somewhat more confusing than numbers.
PLoS ONE, 14(4), e0213522.
https://doi.org/10.1371/jour-
nal.pone.0213522

276. Ancker, J. S., Senathirajah, Y., Kukafka,
R., & Starren, J. B. (2006). Design features of graphs in health risk communication: A systematic review. *Journal of the
American Medical Informatics Association, 13*, 608–618. https://doi.org/
10.1197/jamia.M2115

277. Diefenbach, M. A., Weinstein, N. D., & O'Reilly, J. (1993). Scales for assessing perceptions of health hazard susceptibility. *Health Education Research*, *8*, 181–192. https://doi.org/10.1093/her/8.2.181

278. Wallsten, T. S., Budescu, D. V., Zwick, R., & Kemp, S. M. (1993). Preferences and reasons for communicating probabilistic information in verbal or numerical terms. *Bulletin of the Psychonomic Society*, *31*, 135–138. https://doi.org/10.3758/BF03334162

279. Cokely, E. T., Feltz, A., Ghazal, S., Allan, J. N., Petrova, D., & GarciaRetamero, R. (2017). Decision making skill: From intelligence to numeracy and expertise. In K. A. Ericsson, R. R. Hoffman, A. Kozbelt, & A. M. Williams, (Eds.), *Cambridge handbook of expertise and expert performance*. Cambridge University Press.

280. Butterworth, B. (2010). Foundational numerical capacities and the origins of dyscalculia. *Trends in Cognitive Sciences*, *14*(12), 534–541. https://doi.org/10.1016/j.tics.2010.09.007

281. Butterworth, B., Varma, S., & Laurillard, D. (2011). Dyscalculia: From brain to education. *Science, 332*(6033), 1049–1053. https://doi.org/10.1126/science.1201536

282. Organisation for Economic Cooperation and Development. (2013). *OECD skills outlook 2013: First results from the survey of adult skills*. Organisation for Economic Cooperation and Development Publishing. https://doi.org/10.1787/e11c1c2d-en

283. Organisation for Economic Cooperation and Development. (2013). *Time for the U.S. to reskill?: What the survey of adult skills says*. Organisation for Economic Cooperation and Development Publishing. https://doi.org/10.1787/9789264204904-en

284. Bernhard, A. (2018, July 8). *Why it matters if we become innumerate*. BBC News. https://www.bbc.com/worklife/article/20180706-why-it-matters-if-we-become-innumerate

285. National Numeracy. (n.d.). *What is the issue?* Retrieved November 2nd, 2020 from https://www.nationalnumeracy.org.uk/what-issue

286. Savelli, S., & Joslyn, S. (2013). The advantage of predictive interval forecasts for non-expert users and the impact of visualizations. *Applied Cognitive Psychology*, *27*(4), 527–541. https://doi.org/10.1002/acp.2932

287. Riad, J. K., Norris, F. H., & Ruback, R. B. (1999). Predicting evacuation in two major disasters: Risk perception, social influence, and access to resources. *Journal of Applied Social Psychology*, *29*(5), 918–934. https://doi.org/10.1111/j.1559-1816.1999.tb00132.x

288. Gibbs, L. I., Holloway, C. F. (2013). *Hurricane Sandy after action: Report and recommendations to Mayor Michael R. Bloomberg*. City of New York, New York. https://www1.nyc.gov/assets/housingrecovery/downloads/pdf/2017/sandy_aar_5-2-13.pdf

289. Perry, R. W. (1983). Population evacuation in volcanic eruptions, floods, and nuclear power plant accidents: Some elementary comparisons. *Journal of Community Psychology, 11*(1), 36–47. https://doi.org/10.1002/1520-6629(198301)11:1<36::AID-JCOP2290110104>3.0.CO;2-2

290. Gruntfest, E. C., Downing, T., & White, G. (1978). Big Thompson flood exposes need for better flood reaction system to save lives. *Civil Engineering, 48*, 72–74.

291. Parker D. J., Priest, S. J., & Tapsell, S. M. (2009). Understanding and enhancing the public's behavioural response to flood warning information. *Meteorological Applications, 16*(1), 103– 114. https://doi.org/10.1002/met.119

292. Horney, J. A., MacDonald, P. D., Van Willigen, M., Berke, P. R, & Kaufman, J. S. (2010). Individual actual or perceived property flood risk: Did it predict evacuation from Hurricane Isabel in North Carolina, 2003? *Risk Analysis*, *30*(3), 501–511. https://doi.org/10.1111/j.1539-6924.2009.01341.x

293. Cutter, S. L., & Smith, M. M. (2009). Fleeing from the hurricane's wrath: Evacuation and the two Americas. *Environment: Science and Policy for Sustainable Development*, *51*(2), 26–36. https://doi.org/10.3200/ENVT.51.2.26-36

294. Smith, S. K., & McCarty, C. (2009). Fleeing the storm(s): An examination of evacuation behavior during Florida's 2004 hurricane season. *Demography*, *46*(1), 127–145. https://doi.org/10.1353/dem.0.0048

295. Kahneman, D., & Tversky, A. (1979). Prospect theory: An analysis of decision under risk. *Econometrica*, *47*(2), 263–292. https://doi.org/2307/1914185

296. Betts, S. C., & Taran, Z. (2005). The effects of age and reliability on price in the used car market: A test of prospect theory and multiple reference points. *Proceedings of the Academy of Marketing Studies*, *10*(1), 11–15.

297. Haas M. L. (2001). Prospect theory and the Cuban missile crisis. *International Studies Quarterly*, *45*(2), 241–270. https://doi.org/10.1111/0020-8833.00190

298. LeClerc, J., & Joslyn, S. (2015). The cry wolf effect and weather-related decision making. *Risk Analysis*, *35*(3), 385–395. https://doi.org/10.1111/risa.12336

299. Thompson, C. N., Brommer, D. M., & Sherman-Morris, K. (2012). Pet ownership and the spatial and temporal dimensions of evacuation decisions. *Southeastern Geographer*, *52*(3), 253–266. https://www.jstor.org/stable/26229018?seq=1

300. van Willigen, M., Edwards, T., Edwards, B., & Hessee, S. (2002). Riding out the storm: Experiences of the physically disabled during Hurricanes Bonnie, Dennis, and Floyd. *Natural Hazards Review, 3*(3), 98–106.

301. Spence, P. R., Lachlan, K., Burke, J. M., & Seeger, M. W. (2007). Media use and information needs of the disabled during a natural disaster. *Journal of Health Care for the Poor and Underserved, 18,* 394–404.

302. Fox, M. H., White, G. W., Rooney, C., & Rowland, J. L. (2007). Disaster preparedness and response for persons with mobility impairments. *Journal of Disability Policy Studies, 17*(4), 196–205.

303. White, B. (2006). Disaster relief for deaf persons: Lessons from Hurricanes Katrina and Rita. *The Review of Disability Studies, 2*(3), 49–56. https://scholarspace.manoa.hawaii.edu/bitstream/10125/58269/1/1034.pdf

304. Phillips, B. D., & Morrow, B. H. (2007).
Social science research needs: Focus on
vulnerable populations, forecasting, and
warnings. *Natural Hazards Review, 8*(3),
61–68. https://doi.org/
10.1061/(asce)1527-6988(2007)8:3(61)

305. Rowland, J. L., White, G. W., Fox, M. H.,
& Rooney, C. (2007). Emergency response training practices for people with
disabilities. *Journal of Disability Policy
Studies, 17*(4), 216–222.

306. Barnes, L. R., Gruntfest, E. C., Hayden,
M. H., Schultz, D. M., & Benight, C.
(2007). False alarms and close calls: A conceptual model of warning accuracy.
Weather and Forecasting, 22, 1140–1147.
https://doi.org/1175/WAF1031.1

307. Brooks, H. E., & Correia, J., Jr. (2018).
Long-term performance metrics for Na-
tional Weather Service tornado warnings.
Weather and Forecasting, 33(6),
1501–1511. https://doi.org/10.1175/
WAF-D-18-0120.1

308. Brotzge, J., Erickson, S., & Brooks, H. (2011). A 5-yr climatology of tornado false alarms. *Weather and Forecasting, 26,* 534–544. https://doi.org/10.1175/WAF-D-10-05004.1

309. Trainor, J. E., Nagele, D., Philips, B., & Scott, B. (2015). Tornadoes, social science, and the False Alarm Effect. *Weather, Climate, and Society, 7*(4), 333–352. https://doi.org/10.1175/WCAS-D-14-00052.1

310. Krocak, M. J., Ernst, S., Allan, J. N., Wehde, W., Ripberger, J. T., Silva, C. L., & Jenkins-Smith, H. C. (2020). Thinking outside the polygon: A study of tornado warning perception outside of warning polygon boundaries. *Natural Hazards, 102,* 1351–1368. https://doi.org/10.1007/s11069-020-03970-5

311. Rahn, M., Tomczyk, S., & Schmidt, S. (2020). Storms, fires, and bombs: Analyzing the impact of warning message and receiver characteristics on risk perceptions in different hazards. *Risk Analysis*, early online release. https://doi.org/10.1111/risa.13636

312. Losee, J., Naufel, K. Z., Locker, L., Jr., &
Webster, G. D. (2017). Weather warning
uncertainty: High severity influences
judgement bias. *Weather, Climate, and
Society, 9*(3), 441–454. https://doi.org/
10.1175/WCAS-D-16-0071.1

313. Paul, B. K., Stimers, M., & Caldas, M.
(2014). Predictors of compliance with
tornado warnings issued in Joplin, Missouri, in 2011. *Disasters, 39*(1), 108–124.
https://doi.org/10.1111/disa.12087

314. Wogalter, M. S., & Usher, M. O. (1999).
Effects of concurrent cognitive task load-
ing on warning compliance behavior. *Proceedings of the Human Factors and
Ergonomics Society Annual Meeting,
43*(6), 525–529. https://doi.org/10.1177/
154193129904300612

315. Lee, J. J., Gino, F., & Staats, B. R. (2014).
Rainmakers: Why bad weather means
good productivity. *Journal of Applied Psychology, 99*(3), 504–513. https://nrs.har-
vard.edu/urn-3:HUL.InstRepos:9299650

316. Cornelissen, J. P., & Werner, M. D. (2014). Putting framing in perspective: A review of framing and frame analysis across the management and organizational literature. *Academy of Management Annals, 8*(1), 181–235. https://doi.org/10.5465/19416520.2014.875669

317. Tversky, A., & Kahneman, D. (1981). The framing of decisions and the psychology of choice. *Science, 211*(4481), 453–458. https://doi.org/10.1126/science.7455683

318. Simon, A. F., Fagley, N. S., & Halleran, J. G. (2004). Decision framing: Moderating effects of individual differences and cognitive processing. *Journal of Behavioral Decision Making, 17*(2), 77–93. https://doi.org/10.1002/bdm.463

319. Schuldt, J. P., & Roh, S. (2014). Media frames and cognitive accessibility: What do "global warming" and "climate change" evoke in partisan minds? *Environmental Communication, 8*(4), 529–548. https://doi.org/10.1080/17524032.2014.909510

320. Losee, J. E., & Joslyn, S. (2018). The need to trust: How features of the forecasted weather influence forecast trust. *International Journal of Disaster Risk Reduction*, *30*, 95–104. https://doi.org/10.1016/j.ijdrr.2018.02.032

321. Burgeno, J. N., & Joslyn, S. L. (2020). The impact of weather forecast inconsistency on user trust. *Weather, Climate, and Society*, *12*(4), 679–694. https://doi.org/10.1175/WCAS-D-19-0074.1

322. Allen, D. R., Bolton, M. J., Mogil, H. M., Ault, L. K., Toole, J., & Stewart, A. E. (2020). The "Jim Cantore Effect?" A preliminary test of individual difference-induced media effects upon hurricane evacuation decisions. *PsyArxiv*, preprint. https://doi.org/10.31234/osf.io/2t3sq

323. Mongold, E., Davidson, R. A., Trivedi, J., DeYoung, S., Wachtendorf, T., & Anyidoho, P. (2020). Hurricane evacuation beliefs and behaviour of inland vs. coastal populations. *Environmental Hazards*, early online release. https://doi.org/10.1080/17477891.2020.1829531

324. Sherman-Morris, K., & Lea, A. M. (2016). An exploratory study of the influence of severe weather radar broadcasts. *Journal of Operational Meteorology*, *4*(8), 108–122. https://doi.org/10.15191/nwajom.2016.0408

325. Lang, D., & Benbunan-Fich, R. (2012). The use of social media in disaster situations: Framework and cases. In M. Jennex, (Ed.), *Managing crises and disasters with emerging technologies: Advancements* (pp. 11–24). IGI Global. https://doi.org/10.4018/978-1-4666-0167-3.ch002

326. McGregor, J. D., Elm, J. P., Stark, E. T., Lavan, J., Creel, R., Alberts, C., Woody, C., Ellison, R., & Marshall-Keim, T. (2014). *Best practices in wireless emergency alerts*. Carnegie Melon Software Engineering Institute. https://www.dhs.gov/sites/default/files/publications/Wireless%20Emergency%20Alerts%20Best%20Practices_0.pdf

327. Woody, C., & Ellison, R. (2014). *Maximizing trust in the wireless emergency alerts (WEA) service*. Carnegie Melon Software Engineering Institute. https://www.dhs.gov/sites/default/files/publications/Wireless%20Emergency%20Alerts%20Maximizing%20Trust.pdf

328. Bennett, D. M. (2015). Gaps in wireless emergency alert (WEA) effectiveness. *Public Administration Faculty Publications*, *82*. https://digitalcommons.unomaha.edu/pubadfacpub/82

329. Bean, H., Liu, B. F., Madden, S., Sutton, J., Wood, M. M., & Mileti, D. S. (2016). Disaster warnings in your pocket: How audiences interpret mobile alerts for an unfamiliar audience. *Journal of Contingencies and Crisis Management, 24*(3), 136–147. https://doi.org/10.1111/1468-5973.12108

330. Corley, C. D., Hodas, N. O., Butner, Harrison, J. J., & Berka, C. (2016). *Modeling cognitive response to wireless emergency alerts to inform emergency response interventions.* Pacific Northwest National Laboratory. https://www.dhs.gov/sites/default/files/publications/WEA%20-%20Modeling%20Cognitive%20Response.pdf

331. Bernfield, J. (2020). Obstacles to timely emergency messaging for acute incidents. *Journal of Emergency Management, 18*(5), 425–453. https://www.wm-pllc.org/ojs/index.php/jem/article/view/2821

332. Sutton, J., Renshaw, S. L., Vos, S. C., Olson, M. K., Prestley, R. Gibson, C. B., & Butts, C. T. (2019). Getting the word out, rain or shine: The impact of message features and hazard context on message passing online. *Weather, Climate, and Society*, *11*(4), 763–776. https://doi.org/10.1175/WCAS-D-19-0021.1

333. Sutton, J., & Kuligowski, E. D. (2019). Alerts and warnings on short messaging channels: Guidance from an expert panel process. *Natural Hazards Review*, *20*(2), 04019002. https://doi.org/10.1061/(ASCE)NH.1527-6996.0000324

334. McBride, S. K., Bostrom, A., Sutton, J., de Groot, R. M., Baltray, A. S., Terbush, B., Bodin, P., Dixon, M., Holland, E., Arba, R., Laustsen, P., Liu, S., & Vinci, M. (2020). Developing post-alert messaging for ShakeAlert, the earthquake early warning system for the West Coast of the United States of America. *International Journal of Disaster Risk Reduction*, *50*, 101713. https://doi.org/10.1016/j.ijdrr.2020.101713

335. Sutton, J., Fischer, L., James, L. E., & Cheff, S. E. (2020). Earthquake early warning message testing: Visual attention, behavioral responses, and message perceptions. *International Journal of Disaster Risk Reduction*, 101664. https://doi.org/10.1016/j.ijdrr.2020.101664

336. Friedman, S. M., & Sutton, J. (2020). Evolving coverage of risk in the mass and social media. In H. D. O'Hair, M. J. O'Hair, E. B. Hester, & S. Geegan (Eds.), *The handbook of applied communication research* (pp. 397–416). https://doi.org/10.1002/9781119399926.ch24

337. Sutton, J., & Fischer, L. (2019, June). *Visual risk communication: Attention, understanding, and decision making in response to a changing tornado scenario.* Talk at the 47th Conference on Broadcast Meteorology / 5th Conference on Weather Warnings and Communication, hosted by the American Meteorological Society, San Diego, CA. https://ams.confex.com/ams/47BC5WxComm/meetingapp.cgi/Paper/358568

338. Olson, M. K., Sutton, J., Vos, S. C., Prestley, R., Renshaw, S. L., & Butts, C. T. (2019). Build community before the storm: The National Weather Service's social media engagement. *Journal of Contingencies and Crisis Management, 27*(4), 359–373. https://doi.org/10.1111/1468-5973.12267

339. Renshaw, S. L., Butts, C. T., & Sutton, J. (2020, January). *The social amplification of National Weather Service communication: Impact of audience population factors and message content features.* Talk presented at the 100th Annual Meeting of the American Meteorological Society, Boston, M.A. https://ams.confex.com/ams/2020Annual/meetingapp.cgi/Paper/370437

340. Ali, A., & Ogie, R. (2017). Social media and disasters: Highlighting some wicked problems [Leading Edge]. *IEEE Technology and Society Magazine, 36*(4), 41–43. https://doi.org/10.1109/MTS.2017.2763450

341. Seman, S. (2020). Trusted weather sources and social 'media-rology'. Introductory Meteorology. Retrieved January 28th, 2021 from https://www.e-education.psu.edu/meteo3/node/228

342. Spann, J. (2016). *The 'social media-rologist' dilemma*. AlabamaWx Weather Blog. https://www.alabamawx.com/?p=98058

343. Keller, C., Siegrist, M., & Gutscher, H. (2006). The role of the affect and availability heuristics in risk communication. *Risk Analysis, 26*(3), 631–639. https://doi.org/10.1111/j.1539-6924.2006.00773.x

344. Greening, L., Dollinger, S. J., & Pitz, G. (1996). Adolescents' perceived risk and personal experience with natural disasters: An evaluation of cognitive heuristics. *Acta Psychologica, 91*(1), 27–38. https://doi.org/10.1016/0001-6918(94)00040-9

345. Agans, R. P., & Shaffer, L. S. (1994). The hindsight bias: The role of the availability heuristic and perceived risk. *Basic and Applied Social Psychology, 15*(4), 439–449. https://doi.org/10.1207/s15324834basp1504_3

346. Pachur, T., Hertwig, R., & Steinman, F. (2012). How do people judge risks: Availability heuristic, affect heuristic, or both? *Journal of Experimental Psychology: Applied, 18*(3), 314–330. https://doi.org/1037/a0028279

347. Sunstein, C. R. (2006). The availability heuristic, intuitive cost-benefit analysis, and climate change. *Climatic Change, 77,* 195–210. https://doi.org/10.1007/s10584-006-9073-y

348. Lambrecht, K. M., Hatchett, B. J., Walsh, L. C., Collins, M., & Tolby, Z. (2019). Improving visual communication of weather forecasts with rhetoric. *Bulletin of the American Meteorological Society, 100*(4), 557–563. https://doi.org/10.1175/BAMS-D-18-0186.1

349. Stewart, A. E. (2011). Gulf Coast residents underestimate hurricane destructive potential. *Weather, Climate, and Society, 3*(2), 116–127. https://doi.org/10.1175/2011WCAS1077.1

350. Schumann, R. L., Ash, K. D., & Bowser, G. C. (2018). Tornado warning perception and response: Integrating the roles of visual design, demographics, and hazard experience. *Risk Analysis*, *38*(2), 311–332. https://doi.org/10.1111/risa.12837

351. Sherman-Morris, K., Antonelli, K. B., & Williams, C. C. (2015). Measuring the effectiveness of the graphical communication of hurricane surge threat. *Weather, Climate, and Society*, *7*(1), 69–82. https://doi.org/10.1175/WCAS-D-13-00073.1

352. Boone, A. P., Gunalp, P., & Hegarty, M. (2018). Explicit versus actionable knowledge: The influence of explaining graphical conventions on interpretation of hurricane forecast visualizations. *Journal of Experimental Psychology: Applied*, *24*(3), 275–295. https://doi.org/10.1037/xap0000166

353. Reed, J. R., & Senkbeil, J. C. (2020). Perception and comprehension of the extended forecast graphic: A survey of broadcast meteorologists and the public. *Bulletin of the American Meteorological Society*, *101*(2), E221–E236. https://doi.org/10.1175/BAMS-D-19-0078.1

354. Lenhardt, E. D., Cross, R. N., Krocak, M. J., Ripberger, J. T., Ernst, S. R., Silva, C. L., & Jenkins-Smith, H. C. (2020). How likely is that chance of thunderstorms? A study of how National Weather Service Forecast Offices use words of estimative probability and what they mean to the public. *Journal of Operational Meteorology*, *8*(5), 64–78. https://doi.org/10.15191/nwajom.2020.0805

355. Prestley, R., Olson, M. K., Vos, S. C., & Sutton, J. (2020). Machines, monsters, and coffin corners: Broadcast meteorologists' use of figurative language and intense language during Hurricane Harvey. *Bulletin of the American Meteorological Society*, *101*(8), E1329–E1339. https://doi.org/10.1175/BAMS-D-19-0205.1

356. Long, E. F., Chen, M. K., & Rohla, R. (2020). Political storms: Emergent partisan skepticism of hurricane risks. *Science Advances*, *6*(37), eabb7906. https://doi.org/10.1126/sciadv.abb7906

357. Collins, J., Ersing, R., & Polen, A. (2017). Evacuation decision-making during Hurricane Matthew: An assessment of the effects of social connections. *Weather, Climate, and Society*, *9*(4), 769–776. https://doi.org/10.1175/wcas-d-17-0047.1

358. Bryant, B., Holiner, M., Kroot, R., Sherman-Morris, K., Smylie, W. B., Stryjewski, L., Thomas, M., & Williams, C. I. (2014). Usage of color scales on radar maps. *Journal of Operational Meteorology*, *2*(14), 169–179. https://doi.org/10.15191/nwa-jom.2014.0214

359. Saunders, M. E., Ash, K. D., & Collins, J. M. (2018). Usefulness of the United States National Weather Service radar display as rated by website users. *Weather, Climate, and Society*, *10*(4), 673–691. https://doi.org/10.1175/WCAS-D-17-0108.1

360. Williams, C. A., & Eosco, G. (2020). Is a consistent message achievable? Defining 'message consistency' for weather enterprise researchers and practitioners. *Bulletin of the American Meteorological Society*, *102*(2), E279–295. https://doi.org/10.1175/BAMS-D-18-0250.1

361. Bolton, M. J., & Hanes, S. H. (2020). Improving prejudicial and stigmatized views towards autistic people in the weather enterprise. *National Weather Association Monthly Newsletter, 20*(4). https://doi.org/31234/osf.io/2gstu

362. Bolton, M. J., Mogil, H. M., & Hanes, S. H. (2021). Building bridges: On effective weather communication to, and with, vulnerable populations. *PsyArxiv*, preprint. https://doi.org/10.31234/osf.io/kx64f

363. Bolton, M. J., Wise, G., & Blumberg, W. G. (2016, June). *Color blindness in the weather enterprise: Discussion and a look at solutions*. Talk at the 44th Conference on Broadcast Meteorology hosted by the American Meteorological Society, Austin, TX. https://ams.confex.com/ams/44Broadcast/webprogram/Paper295309.html.

364. Sherman-Morris, K., Pechacek, T., Griffin, D. J., & Sekbeil, J. (2020). Tornado warning awareness, information needs and the barriers to protective action of individuals who are blind. *International Journal of Disaster Risk Reduction, 50,* 101709. https://doi.org/10.1016/j.ijdrr.2020.101709

365. Senkbeil, J. C., Griffin, D. J., Sherman-Morris, K., Saari, J., & Brothers, K. (2021). Improving tornado warning communication for Deaf and hard of hearing audiences. *Journal of Operational Meteorology, 9*(2), 18–35. https://doi.org/10.15191/nwajom.2021.0902

366. Cools, M., & Creemers, L. (2013). The dual role of weather forecasts on changes in activity-travel behavior. *Journal of Transport Geography, 28,* 167–175. https://doi.org/10.1016/j.jtrangeo.2012.11.002

367. Hoogendoorn, R. G., Tamminga, G., Hoogendoorn, S. P., & Daamen, W. (2010). Longitudinal driving behavior under adverse weather conditions: adaptation effects, model performance and freeway capacity in case of fog. *Proceedings of the 13th International IEEE Conference on Intelligent Transportation Systems*. https://doi.org/10.1109/itsc.2010.5625046

368. Cools, M., Moons, E., & Wets, G. (2010). Assessing the impact of weather on traffic intensity. *Weather, Climate, and Society*, *2*(1), 60–68. https://doi.org/10.1175/2009wcas1014.1

369. Kilpeläinen, M., & Summala, H. (2007). Effects of weather and weather forecasts on driver behaviour. *Transportation Research Part F: Traffic Psychology and Behaviour*, *10*(4), 288–299. https://doi.org/10.1016/j.trf.2006.11.002

370. Meng, M., Zhang, J., Wong, Y. D., & Au,
P. H. (2016). Effect of weather conditions
and weather forecast on cycling travel behavior in Singapore. *International Journal
of Sustainable Transportation, 10*(9),
773–780. https://doi.org/10.1080/
15568318.2016.1149646

371. Ahmed, F., Rose, G., & Jakob, C. (2013).
Commuter cyclist travel behavior. *Transportation Research Record: Journal of the
Transportation Research Board, 2387*(1),
76–82. https://doi.org/10.3141/2387-09

372. Jeuring, J. H. G. (2017). Weather perceptions, holiday satisfaction and perceived
attractiveness of domestic vacationing in
The Netherlands. *Tourism Management,
61*, 70–81. https://doi.org/10.1016/
j.tourman.2017.01.018

373. Lohmann, M., & Hübner, A. C. (2013).
Tourist behavior and weather. *Mondes
Du Tourisme, 8*, 44–59. https://doi.org/
10.4000/tourisme.83

374. Matzarakis, A. (2006). Weather- and climate-related information for tourism.
*Tourism and Hospitality Planning & De-
velopment, 3*(2), 99–115. https://doi.org/
10.1080/14790530600938279

375. De Freitas, C. R. (2003). Tourism climatology: Evaluating environmental information for decision making and business planning in the recreation and tourism sector. *International Journal of Biometeorology, 48*(1), 45–54. https://doi.org/10.1007/s00484-003-0177-z

376. Steiger, R., Abegg, B., & Jänicke, L. (2016). Rain, rain, go away, come again another day. Weather preferences of summer tourists in mountain environments. *Atmosphere, 7*(5), 63. https://doi.org/10.3390/atmos7050063

377. Wilhelm Stanis, S., & Barbieri, C. (2013). Niche tourism attributes scale: A case of storm chasing. *Current Issues in Tourism, 16*(5), 495–500. https://doi.org/10.1080/13683500.2012.733360

378. Robertson, D. (2010). Beyond *Twister*: A geography of recreational storm chasing on the Southern Plains. *Geographical Review, 89*(4), 533–553. https://doi.org/10.1111/j.1931-0846.1999.tb00233.x

379. Boulais, C. M. (2017). When severe weather becomes a tourist attraction: Understanding the relationship with nature in storm-chasing tourism. *Weather, Climate, and Society, 9*(3), 367–376. https://doi.org/10.1175/WCAS-D-16-0038.1

380. Xu, S., Barbieri, C., Wilhelm Stanis, S., & Market, P. S. (2012). Sensation-seeking attributes associated with storm chasing tourists: Implications for future engagement. *International Journal of Tourism Research, 14*, 269–284. https://doi.org/10.1002/jtr.860

381. Ludlum, D. (1984). *The weather factor*. Houghton Mifflin.

382. Andrews, W. (1966). American voting participation. *The Western Political Quarterly, 19*, 639–652.

383. Gomez, B. T., Hansford, T. G., & Krause, G. A. (2007). The Republicans should pray for rain: Weather, turnout, and voting in U.S. presidential elections. *The Journal of Politics, 69*(3), 649–663.

384. Bassi, A. (2013). Weather, mood, and voting: An experimental analysis of the effect of weather beyond turnout. https://doi.org/10.2139/ssrn.2273189

385. Gatrell, J. D., & Bierly, G. D. (2002). Weather and voter turnout: Kentucky primary and general elections, 1990-2000. *Southeastern Geographer, 42*(1), 114–134. https://doi.org/10.1353/sgo.2002.0007

386. Fraga, B., & Hersh, E. (2011). Voting costs and voter turnout in competitive elections. *Quarterly Journal of Political Science, 5*(4), 339–356. https://doi.org/10.1561/100.00010093

387. Knack, S. (1994). Does rain help the Republicans? Theory and evidence on turnout and the vote. *Public Choice, 79,* 187–209. https://doi.org/10.1007/BF01047926

388. Shachar, R., & Nalebuff, B. (1999). Follow the leader: Theory and evidence on political participation. *The American Economic Review*, *89*, 525–547

389. Eisinga, R., Te Grotenhuis, M., & Pelzer, B. (2011). Weather conditions and voter turnout in Dutch national parliament elections, 1971–2010. *International Journal of Biometeorology*, *56*(4), 783–786. https://doi.org/10.1007/s00484-011-0477-7

390. Grant, A. M., & Schwartz, B. (2011). Too much of a good thing: The challenge and opportunity of the inverted U. *Perspectives on Psychological Science*, *6*(1), 61–76. https://doi.org/10.1177/1745691610393523

391. Persson, M., Sundell, A., & Öhrvall, R. (2014). Does Election Day weather affect voter turnout? Evidence from Swedish elections. *Electoral Studies*, *33*, 335–342. https://doi.org/10.1016/j.electstud.2013.07.021

392. Hirshleifer, D., & Shumway, T. (2003). Good day sunshine: Stock returns and the weather. *The Journal of Finance, 58*(3), 1009–1032. https://doi.org/10.1111/1540-6261.00556

393. Saunders, Jr., E. M. (1993). Stock prices and Wall Street weather. *The American Economic Review, 83*(5), 1337–1345. https://www.jstor.org/stable/2117565

394. Trombley, M. A. (1997). Stock prices and Wall Street weather: Additional evidence. *Quarterly Journal of Business and Economics, 36*(3), 11–21. https://www.jstor.org/stable/40473319

395. Andrikopoulos, A., Wang, C., & Zheng, M. (2019). Is there still a weather anomaly? An investigation of stock and foreign exchange markets. *Finance Research Letters, 30*, 51–59. https://doi.org/10.1016/j.frl.2019.03.026

396. Murray, K. B., Di Muro, F., Finn, A., & Popkowski Leszczyc, P. (2010). The effect of weather on consumer spending. *Journal of Retailing and Consumer Services, 17*(6), 512–520. https://doi.org/10.1016/j.jretconser.2010.08.006

397. Parsons, A. G. (2001). The association between daily weather and daily shopping patterns. *Australasian Marketing Journal*, *9*(2), 78–84.

398. Di Nicola, M., Mazza, M., Panaccione, I., Moccia, L., Giuseppin, G., Marano, G., Grandinetti, P., Camardese, G., De Berardis, D., Pompili, M., & Janiri, L. (2020). Sensitivity to climate and weather changes in euthymic bipolar subjects: Association with suicide attempts. *Frontiers in Psychiatry*, *11*(95). https://doi.org/10.3389/fpsyt.2020.00095

399. Balsamo, V., Sirtori, P. G., Miani, A., Jr., Di Francesco, A., Franceschini, R., Mauro, F., Alberti, G., & Grassi, G. (1992). Meteoropathy: A syndrome continuously on the increase. *La Clinica Terapeutica*, *141*(7), 3–8.

400. Bellini, S., Migliorati, M., Ricci, F., Erbuto, D., & Pompili, M. (2015). The association between meteoropathy, depression, hopelessness and quality of life in medication-overuse headache patients. *The Journal of Headache and Pain*, *16*(1), A50. https://doi.org/10.1186/1129-2377-16-S1-A50

401. Mazza, M., Di Nicola, M., Catalano, V., Callea, A., Martinotti, G., Harnic, D., Bruschi, A., Battaglia, C., & Janiri, L. (2012). Description and validation of a questionnaire for the detection of meteoropathy and meteorosensitivity: The METEO-Q. *Comprehensive Psychiatry*, *53*, 103–106. https://doi.org/10.1016/j.comppsych.2011.02.002

402. Oniszczenko, W. (2020). Affective temperaments and meteoropathy among women: A cross-sectional study. *PLoS ONE*, *15*(5), e0232725. https://doi.org/10.1371/journal.pone.0232725

403. Latman, N. S. (1987). Influence of atmospheric factors on the rheumatic diseases. *Experientia*, *43*, 32–38. https://doi.org/10.1007/BF01940350

404. Shutty, M. S., Cundiff, G., & DeGood, D. E. (1992). Pain complaint and the weather: Weather sensitivity and symptom complaints in chronic pain patients. *Pain*, *49*, 199–204. https://doi.org/10.1016/0304-3959(92)90143-Y

405. Dequeker, J., & Wuestenrand, L. (1986). The effect of biometeorological factors on Ritchie Articular Index and pain in rheumatoid arthritis. *Scandinavian Journal of Rheumatology, 15*, 280–284. https://doi.org/10.3109/03009748609092593

406. Guedj, D., & Weinberger, A. (1990). Effect of weather conditions on rheumatic patients. *Annals of the Rheumatic Diseases, 49*(3), 158–159. https://doi.org/1136/ard.49.3.158

407. Affleck, G., Pfeiffer, G., Tennen, H., & Fifield, J. (1987). Attributional processes in rheumatoid arthritis patients. *Arthritis & Rheumatism, 30*(8), 927–931. https://doi.org/10.1002/art.1780300813

408. Strusberg, I., Mendelberg, R. C., Serra, H. A., & Strusberg, A. M. (2002). Influence of weather conditions on rheumatic pain. *The Journal of Rheumatology, 29*(2), 335–338.

409. Patberg, W. R., Neinhuis, R. L., Vergina, F. (1985). Relation between meteorological factors and pain in rheumatoid arthritis in a marine climate. *Journal of Rheumatology, 12,* 711–715.

410. Jamison, R. N., Anderson, K. O., & Slater, M. A. (1995). Weather changes and pain: Perceived influence of local climate on pain complaint in chronic pain patients. *Pain, 61*(2), 309–315. https://doi.org/10.1016/0304-3959(94)00215-Z

411. Inoue, S., Kobayashi, F., Nishihara, M.,, Arai, Y.-C. P., Ikemoto, T., Kawai, T., Inoue, M., Hasegawa, T., & Ushida, T. (2015). Chronic pain in the Japanese community–prevalence, characteristics and impact on quality of life. *PLoS ONE, 10*(6), e0129262. https://doi.org/10.1371/journal.pone.0129262

412. Vergés, J., Montell, E., Tomàs, E., Cumelles, G., Castañeda, G., Marti, N., & Möller, I. (2004). Weather conditions can influence rheumatic diseases. *Proceedings of the Western Pharmacology Society, 47,* 134–136.

413. Hagglund, K. J., Deuser, W. E., Buckelew, S. P., Hewett, J., & Kay, D. R. (1994). Weather, beliefs about weather, and disease severity among patients with fibromyalgia. *Arthritis & Rheumatism*, *7*(3), 130–135. https://doi.org/10.1002/art.1790070306

414. Miranda, L., Parente, M., Silva, C., Clemente-Coelho, P., Santos, H., Cortes, S., Medeiros, D., Ribeiro, J. S., Barcelos, F., Sousa, M., Miguel, C., Figueiredo, R., Mediavilla, M., Simões, E., Silva, M., Patto, J. V., Madeira, H., Ferreira, J., Micaelo, M., ... Teixeira, A. (2007). Perceived pain and weather changes in rheumatic patients. *Acta Reumatologica Portuguesa*, *32*(4), 351–361.

415. Ng, J., Scott, D., Taneja, A., Gow, P., & Gosai, A. (2004). Weather changes and pain in rheumatology patients. *APLAR Journal of Rheumatology*, *7*(3), 204–206. https://doi.org/10.1111/j.1479-8077.2004.00099.x

416. Croitoru, A.-E., Dogaru, G., Man, T. C., Mălăescu, S., Motricală, M., & Scripcă, A. (2019). Perceived influence of weather conditions on rheumatic pain in Romania. *Advances in Meteorology*, 9187105. https://doi.org/10.1155/2019/9187105

417. von Mackensen, S., Hoeppe, P., Maarouf, A., Tourigny, P., & Nowak, D. (2005). Prevalence of weather sensitivity in Germany and Canada. *International Journal of Biometeorology*, *49*, 156–166. https://doi.org/10.1007/s00484-004-0226-2

418. Timmermans, E. J., van der Pas, S., Schaap, L. A., Sánchez-Martinez, M., Zambon, S., Peter, R., Pedersen, N. L., Dennison, E. M., Denkinger, M., Castell, M. V., Siviero, P., Herbolsheimer, F., Edwards, M. H., Otero, A., & Deeg, D. J. H. (2014). Self-perceived weather sensitivity and joint pain in older people with osteoarthritis in six European countries: Results from the European Project on OSteoArthritis (EPOSA). *BMC Musculoskelatal Disorders, 15*, 66. https://doi.org/10.1186/1471-2474-15-66

419. Wu, Y.-T., Luben, R., Wareham, N., Griffin, S., & Jones, A. P. (2017). Weather, day length and physical activity in older adults: Cross-sectional results from the European Prospective Investigation into Cancer and Nutrition (EPIC) Norfolk Cohort. *PLoS ONE, 12*(5), e0177767. https://doi.org/10.1371/journal.pone.0177767

420. Klenk, J., Büchele, G., Rapp, K., Franke, S., Peter, R., & the ActiFE Study Group. (2012). Walking on sunshine: Effect of weather conditions on physical activity in older people. *Journal of Epidemiology & Community Health*, *66*(5), 474–476. https://doi.org/10.1136/jech.2010.128090

421. King, E. A., Fleschler, R. G., & Cohen, S. M. (1997). Association between significant decrease in barometric pressure and onset of labor. *Journal of Midwifery and Women's Health*, *42*(1), 32–34. http://doi.org/1016/S0091-2182(96)00101-2

422. Noller, K. L., Resseguie, L. J., & Voss, V. (1996). The effect of changes in atmospheric pressure on the occurrence of the spontaneous onset of labor in term pregnancies. *American Journal of Obstetrics and Gynecology*, *174*(4), 1192–1199. https://doi.org/10.1016/s0002-9378(96)70661-0

423. Driscoll, D. M., & Merker, D. G. (1984). A search for associations between weather and the onset of human parturition. *International Journal of Biometeorology, 28*, 211–224. https://doi.org/10.1007/BF02187961

424. Yackerson, N., Piura, B., & Sheiner, E. (2008). The influence of meteorological factors on the emergence of preterm delivery and preterm premature rupture of membrane. *Journal of Perinatology, 28*, 707–711.

425. Newton-Smith, W. H. (2000). *A companion to the philosophy of science*. Blackwell.

426. National Research Council. (2002). *Scientific research in education*. The National Academies Press. https://doi.org/10.17226/10236.

427. Merton, R. K. (1973). *The sociology of science: Theoretical and empirical investigations*. University of Chicago Press.

428. Silberman, S. (2019, 24 September). *Greta Thunberg became a climate activist not in spite of her autism, but because of it.* Vox. https://www.vox.com/first-person/2019/5/6/18531551/greta-thunberg-autism-aspergers

429. Thunberg, G., Thunberg, S., Ernman, M., & Ernman, B. (2020). *Our house is on fire: Scenes of a family and a planet in crisis.* Penguin Books.

430. D. E. (1984). Explaining negativity biases in evaluation and choice behavior: Theory and research. In T. C. Kinnear, (Ed.), *NA – Advances in Consumer Research Volume 11* (pp. 703–708). Association for Consumer Research. http://acrwebsite.org/volumes/6335/volumes/v11/NA-11

431. Ito, T. A., Larsen, J. T., Kyle Smith, N., & Cacioppo, J. T. (1998). Negative information weighs more heavily on the brain: The negativity bias in evaluative categorizations. *Journal of Personality and Social Psychology, 75*(4), 887–900.

432. Smith, N. K., Larsen, J. T., Chartrand, T. L., Cacioppo, J. T., Katafiasz, H. A., & Moran, K. E. (2006). Being bad isn't always good: Affective context moderates the attention bias toward negative information. *Journal of Personality and Social Psychology*, *90*(2), 210–220. https://doi.org/10.1037/0022-3514.90.2.210

433. Siegrist, M., & Cvetkovich, G. (2001). Better negative than positive? Evidence of a bias for negative information about possible health dangers. *Risk Analysis*, *21*(1), 199–206.

434. Hilbig, H. E. (2009). Sad, thus true. Negativity bias in judgments of truth. *Journal of Experimental Social Psychology*, *45*(4), 983–986. https://doi.org/10.1016/j.jesp.2009.04.012

435. Baumeister, R. F., Bratslavsky, E., Finkenauer, C., & Vohs, K. D. (2001). Bad is stronger than good. *Review of General Psychology*, *5*(4), 323–370. https://doi.org/10.1037//1089-2680.5.4.323

436. Gazzo Castañeda, L. E., Richter, B., & Knauff, M. (2015). Negativity bias in defeasible reasoning. *Thinking & Reasoning, 22*(2), 209–220. https://dioi.org/10.1080/13546783.2015.1117988

437. Hansen L. K., Arvidsson, A., Nielsen, F. A., Colleoni, E., & Etter, M. (2011). Good friends, bad news - affect and virality in Twitter. In Park, J. J., Yang, L. T., Lee, C., (Eds.), *Future information technology. Communications in computer and information science, volume 185.* Springer, Berlin, Heidelberg.

438. Bebbington, K., MacLeod, C., Ellison, T. M., & Fay, N. (2017). The sky is falling: Evidence of a negativity bias in the social transmission of information. *Evolution and Human Behavior, 38*(1), 92–101. https://doi.org/10.1016/j.evolhumbehav.2016.07.004

439. Soroka, S., Fournier, P., & Nir, L. (2019). Cross-national evidence of a negativity bias in psychophysiological reactions to news. *Proceedings of the National Academies of Science, 116*(38), 18888–188892. https://doi.org/10.1073/pnas.1908369116

440. Wang, S., Corner, A., Chapman, D., & Markowitz, E. (2018). Public engagement with climate imagery in a changing digital landscape. *Wiley Interdisciplinary Reviews: Climate Change*, *9*(2), e509. https://doi.org/10.1002/wcc.509

441. Nerlich, B., Koteyko, N., & Brown, B. (2010). Theory and language of climate change communication. *Wiley Interdisciplinary Reviews: Climate Change*, *1*(1), 97–110. https://doi.org/10.1002/wcc.2

442. Boykoff, M., & Boykoff, J. (2004). Balance as bias: Global warming and the US prestige press *Global Environmental Change*, *14*, 125–136.

443. Boykoff, M. T. (2007). Flogging a dead norm? Newspaper coverage of anthropogenic climate change in the USA and UK from 2003-2006. *Area*, *39*(4), 470-481.

444. Boykoff, M. (2008). Media and scientific communication: A case of climate change. In D. G. E Liverman, C. P. G. Pereira, & B. Marker, (Eds.), *Communicating environmental geoscience* (pp. 11–18). Geological Society of London.

445. Boykoff, M. T., & Rajan, S. R. (2007). *Signals and noise: Mass media coverage of climate change in the USA and the UK.* European Molecular Biology Organisation Reports, *8*(3), 207–211.

446. Beckett, C., & Deuze, M. (2016). On the role of emotion in the future of journalism. *Social Media + Society*, *2*(3), 205630511666239. https://doi.org/10.1177/2056305116662395

447. Peters, C. (2011). Emotion aside or emotional aside? Crafting an 'experience of involvement' in the news. *Journalism*, *12*(3), 297–316. https://doi.org/10.1177/1464884910388224

448. de los Santos, T. M., & Nabi, R. L. (2019). Emotionally charged: Exploring the role of emotion in online news information seeking and processing. *Journal of Broadcasting and Electronic Media*, *63*(1), 39–58. https://doi.org/10.1080/08838151.2019.1566861

449. Klemm, C., Hartmann, T., & Das, E.
(2017). Fear-mongering or fact-driven? Il-
luminating the interplay of objective risk
and emotion-evoking form in the response to epidemic news. *Health Communication*, *34*(1), 74–83. https://doi.org/
10.1080/10410236.2017.1384429

450. Kim, H., Cameron, G. T. (2011). Emotions matter in crisis: The role of anger
and sadness in the publics' response to crisis news framing and corporate crisis response. *Communication Research*, *38*(6),
826–855. https://doi.org/
10.11770093650210385813

451. Maier, S., Slovic, P., & Mayorga, M.
(2017). Reader reaction to news of mass
suffering: Assessing the influence of story
form and emotional response. *Journalism*,
18(8), 1011–1029. https://doi.org/
10.11771464884916663597

452. Meldrum, H., Szymanski, D., Oches, E. A., & Davis, P. T. (2017). Speaking out or staying quiet on climate change: Broadcast meteorologists influenced by the need to be pithy, popular, and politically cautious. In W. F. Leal, & J. Keenan, (Eds.), *Climate change adaptation in North America* (pp. 261–277). Climate change management. Springer, Cham. https://doi.org/10.1007/978-3-319-53742-9_16

453. Wilson, K. (2009). Opportunities and obstacles for television weathercasters to report on climate change. *Bulletin of the American Meteorological Society, 90*(10), 1457–1465. https://doi.org/10.1175/2009bams2947.1

454. Zhao, X., Maibach, E., Gandy, J., Witte, J., Cullen, H., Klinger, B. A., Rowan, K. E., Witte, A., & Pyle, A. (2014). Climate change education through TV weathercasts: Results of a field experiment. *Bulletin of the American Meteorological Society, 95*(1), 117–130. https://doi.org/10.1175/BAMS-D-12-00144.1

455. Timm, K. M. F., Perkins, D., Myers, T., Placky Woods, B., & Maibach, E. W. (2020). Reporting on climate change by broadcast meteorologists: A national assessment. *Bulletin of the American Meteorological Society*, *101*(2), E129–E140. https://doi.org/10.1175/BAMS-D-18-0225.1

456. Placky Woods, B., Maibach, E., Witte, J., Ward, B., Seitter, K., Gardiner, N., Herring, D., & Cullen, H. (2016). Climate Matters: A comprehensive educational resource program for broadcast meteorologists. *Bulletin of the American Meteorological Society*, *97*(5), 709–712. https://doi.org/10.1175/BAMS-D-14-00235.1

457. Maibach, E., Mazzone, R., Drost, R., Myers, T., Sietter, K., Hayhoe, K., Ryan, B., Witte, J., Gardiner, N., Hassol, S., Lazo, J. K., Placky, B., Sublette, S., & Cullen, H. (2017). TV weathercasters' views of climate change appear to be rapidly evolving. *Bulletin of the American Meteorological Society*, *98*(10), 2061–2064. https://doi.org/10.1175/BAMS-D-15-00206.1

458. Moser, S. C. (2007). More bad news: The risk of neglecting emotional responses to climate change information. In S. C. Moser & L. Dilling (Eds.), *Creating a climate for change* (pp. 64–80). Cambridge University Press.

459. Lertzman, R. (2017, September 18). *Tackling apathy and denial*. Climate2020. https://www.climate2020.org.uk/tackling-apathy-denial/

460. Schinko, T. (2020). Overcoming political climate-change apathy in the era of #FridaysForFuture. *One Earth*, *2*(1), 20–23. https://doi.org/10.1016/j.oneear.2019.12.012

461. Mildenberger, M., & Lieserowitz, A. (2017). Public opinion on climate change: Is there an economy-environment tradeoff? *Environmental Politics*, *26*(5), 801–824. https://doi.org/10.1080/09644016.2017.1322275

462. Elliott, E., Seldon, B., & Regens, J. (1997). Political and economic determinants of individuals' support for environmental spending. *Journal of Environmental Management, 51*(1), 15–27. https://doi.org/10.1006/jema.1996.0129

463. Inglehart, R. (1997). *Modernization and postmodernization*. Cambridge University Press.

464. Guber, D. (2003). *The grassroots of a green revolution: Polling America on the environment*. MIT Press.

465. Kahn, M., & Kotchen M. (2011). Business cycle effects on concern about climate change: The chilling effect of recession. *Climate Change Economics, 2*(3), 257–273. https://doi.org/10.1142/S2010007811000292

466. Scruggs, L., & Benegal, S. (2012). Declining public concern about climate change: Can we blame the great recession? *Global Environmental Change, 22*(2), 505–515. https://doi.org/10.1016/j.gloenvcha.2012.01.002

467. Shum, R. (2012). Effects of economic recession and local weather on climate change attitudes. *Climate Policy*, *12*(1), 38–49. https://doi.org/10.1080/14693062.2011.579316

468. Brulle, R., Carmichael, K., & Jenkins, J. (2012). Shifting public opinion on climate change: An empirical assessment of factors influencing concern over climate change in the US, 2002-2010. *Climatic Change*, *114*(2), 169–188. https://doi.org/10.1007/s10584-012-0403-y

469. Carmichael, J., & Brulle, R. (2017). Elite cues, media coverage, and public concern: An integrated path analysis of public opinion on climate change, 2001-2013. *Environmental Politics*, *26*(2), 232–252. https://doi.org/10.1080/09644016.2016.1263433

470. Maslow, A. (1954). *Motivation and personality*. Harpers.

471. Kaufman, S. B. (2020). *Transcend: The new science of self-actualization*. Tarcher-Perigee.

472. Weber, E. (2010). What shapes perceptions of climate change? *WIRE: Climate Change*, *1*(3), 332–342.

473. Onion, R. (2019, September 9). *How Greta Thunberg captured our attention on climate*. Slate. https://slate.com/technology/2019/09/greta-thunberg-climate-activism-scares-the-right-and-the-left.html

474. Grove, R., Roth, I., & Hoekstra, R. A. (2016). The motivation for special interests in individuals with autism and controls: Development and validation of the Special Interest Motivation Scale. *Autism Research*, *9*(6), 677–688. https://doi.org/10.1002/aur.1560

475. Grove, R., Hoekstra, R. A., Wierda, M., & Begeer, S. (2018). Special interests and subjective wellbeing in autistic adults. *Autism Research*, *11*(5), 766–775. https://doi.org/10.1002/aur.1931

476. Robinson, J. F., & Vitale, L. J. (1954). Children with circumscribed interest patterns. *American Journal of Orthopsychiatry*, *24*(4), 755–766. https://doi.org/10.1111/j.1939-0025.1954.tb06145.x

477. Silberman, S. (2015). *Neurotribes: The legacy of autism and the future of neurodiversity*. Avery.

478. Wood, R. (2019). Autism, intense interests and support in school: From wasted efforts to shared understandings. *Educational Review*. Early online release. https://doi.org/10.1080/00131911.2019.1566213

479. Grandin, T. (2006). *Thinking in pictures: My life with autism*. Vintage Books.

480. Roser-Renouf, C., Maibach, E. W., Leiserowitz, A., & Zhao, X. (2014). The genesis of climate change activism: From key beliefs to political action. *Climatic Change, 125*, 163–178. https://doi.org/10.1007/s10584-014-1173-5

481. Bogdan, I. V., & King, B. G. (2012). Social movements, risk perceptions, and economic outcomes: The effect of primary and secondary stakeholder activism on firms perceived environmental risk and financial performance. *American Sociological Review, 77*(4), 573–596. https://doi.org/10.1177/0003122412448796

482. McAdam, D. (2017). Social movement
theory and the prospects for climate
change activism in the United States. *Annual Review of Political Science, 20*,
189–208. https://doi.org/10.1146/an-
nurev-polisci-052615-025801

483. Steentjes, K., Kurz, T., Barreto, M., &
Morton, T. A. (2017). The norms associated with climate change: Understanding
social norms through acts of interpersonal
activism. *Global Environmental Change,
43*, 116–125. https://doi.org/10.1016/
j.gloenvcha.2017.01.008

484. Marlon, J. R., Bloodhart, B., Ballew, M.
T., Rolfe-Redding, J., Roser-Renouf, C.,
Leiserowitz, A., & Maibach, E. (2019).
How hope and doubt affect climate
change mobilization. *Frontiers in Communication, 4*, 20. https://doi.org/
10.3389/fcomm.2019.00020

485. Nairn, K. (2019). Learning from young
people engaged in climate activism: The
potential of collectivizing despair and
hope. *Young, 27*(5), 435–450.
https://doi.org/10.1177/
1103308818817603

486. Gunningham, N. (2019). Averting climate catastrophe: Environmental activism, Extinction Rebellion and coalitions of influence. *King's Law Journal, 30*(2), 194–202. https://doi.org/10.1080/09615768.2019.1645424

487. Chersich, M. F., Scorgie, F., Wright, C. Y., Mullick, S., Mathee, A., Hess, J., Richter, M., & Rees, H. (2019). Climate change and adolescents in South Africa: The role of youth activism and the health sector in safeguarding adolescents' health and education. *South African Medical Journal, 109*(9), 615–619. https://doi.org/10.7196/samj.2019.v109i9.14327

488. Stott, R., Smith, R., Williams, R., & Godlee, F. (2019). Schoolchildren's activism is a lesson for health professionals. *BMJ, 365*, l1938. https://doi.org/10.1136/bmj.l1938

489. Vavilov, E. M. (2019). *Lessons about activism from a Swedish high school student: A rhetorical analysis of Greta Thunberg's public speeches on climate change.* Unpublished Master's thesis, Jönköping University. https://www.diva-portal.org/smash/record.jsf?pid=diva2%3A1353725&dswid=-5772

490. de Moor, J., De Vydt, M., Uba, K., & Wahlström, M. (2020). New kids on the block: Taking stock of the recent cycle of climate activism. *Social Movement Studies.* Early online release. https://doi.org/10.1080/14742837.2020.1836617

491. Dobson, J. (2019). Youth activism for health: Taking the future into their own hands. *BMJ, 367,* l6881. https://doi.org/10.1136/bmj.l6881

492. O'Brien, K., Selboe, E., & Hayward, B. M. (2018). Exploring youth activism on climate change: Dutiful, disruptive, and dangerous dissent. *Ecology and Society, 23*(4), 42. https://doi.org/10.5751/ES-10287-230342

493. Murray, S. (2020). *Framing a climate crisis: A descriptive framing analysis of how Greta Thunberg inspired the masses to take to the streets.* Unpublished Bachelor's thesis, Uppsala University. https://www.diva-portal.org/smash/record.jsf?pid=diva2%3A1386491&dswid=-404

494. Ballew, M. T., Goldberg, M. H., Rosenthal, S. A., Cutler, M. J., & Leiserowitz, A. (2019). Climate change activism among Latino and White Americans. *Frontiers in Communication, 3*, 58. https://doi.org/10.3389/fcomm.2018.00058

495. Rogers, C. R. (1995). *On becoming a person: A therapist's view of psychotherapy.* Houghton Mifflin.

496. Polanyi, M. (2015). *Personal knowledge: Towards a post-critical philosophy (Enlarged edition).* University of Chicago Press.

497. Capstick, S. B., & Pidgeon, N. F. (2014). Public perception of cold weather events as evidence for and against climate change. *Climatic Change, 122*, 695–708. https://doi.org/10.1007/s10584-013-1003-1

498. Leiserowitz, A., Maibach, E., Roser-Renouf, C., & Hmielowski, J. D. (2012). *Global warming's six Americas, March 2012 & November 2011.* Yale Project on Climate Change Communication. http://environment.yale.edu/climate/files/Six-Americas-March-2012.pdf

499. Smith N, & Leiserowitz, A. (2012) The rise of global warming skepticism: Exploring affective image associations in the United States over time. *Risk Analysis, 32,* 1021–1032

500. Durran, D. R. (2020). Can the issuance of hazardous-weather warnings inform the attribution of extreme events to climate change? *Bulletin of the American Meteorological Society, 101*(8), E1452–E1463. https://doi.org/10.1175/BAMS-D-20-0026.1

501. Capstick, S. B. (2012) *Climate change discourses in use by the UK public: commonalities and variations over a fifteen year period.* Doctoral dissertation, Cardiff University. http://orca.cf.ac.uk/24182/

502. Van der Linden, S. (2015). A conceptual critique of the cultural cognition thesis. *Science Communication*, *38*(1), 128–138. https://doi.org/10.1177/1075547015614970

503. Kahan, D. M., Braman, D., Gastil, J., Slovic, P., & Mertz, C. K. (2007). Culture and identity-protective cognition: Explaining the white male effect in risk perception. *Journal of Empirical Legal Studies*, *4*(3), 465–505. http://papers.ssrn.com/abstract=995634

504. McNeeley, S. M., & Lazrus, H. (2014). The cultural theory of risk for climate change adaptation. *Weather, Climate, and Society*, *6*, 504–519. https://doi.org/1175/WCAS-D-13-00027.1

505. Kahan, D. M., Peters, E., Wittlin, M., Slovic, P., Ouellette, L. L., Braman, D., & Mandel, G. (2012). The polarizing impact of science literacy and numeracy on perceived climate change risks. *Nature Climate Change*, *2*, 732–735 https://doi.org/10.1038/nclimate1547

506. Kahan, D. M. (2010). Fixing the communications failure. *Nature*, *463*, 296-297.

507. Persson, J., Sahlin, N.-E., & Wallin, A.
      (2015). Climate change, values, and the
      cultural cognition thesis. *Environmental
      Science & Policy, 52*, 1–5. https://doi.org/
      10.1016/j.envsci.2015.05.001

508. Leiserowitz, A. A. (2005). American risk
      perceptions: Is climate change dangerous?
      Risk Analysis, 25(6), 1433–1442.
      https://doi.org/10.1111/
      j.1540-6261.2005.00690.x

509. Rosenbaum, A. (2018, October 31). *Personal space and American individualism.*
      Brown Political Review. https://brown-
      politicalreview.org/2018/10/personal-
      space-american-individualism/

510. Dunlap, R. E., & Allen, M. P. (1976). Partisan difference on environmental issues:
      A Congressional roll-call analysis. *Western Political Quarterly, 49*, 384–397.

511. Kenski, H. C., & Kenski, M. C. (1980).
      Partisanship, ideology, and constituency
      differences on environmental issues in the
      U.S. House of Representatives: 1973-78.
      Policy Studies Journal, 9(3), 325–335.
      https://doi.org/10.1111/
      j.1541-0072.1980.tb00942.x

512. Dunlap, R. E., & McCright, A. M. (2008). A widening gap: Republican and Democratic views on climate change. *Environment: Science and Policy for Sustainable Development, 50*(5), 26–35. https://doi.org/10.3200/ENVT.50.5.26-35

513. Swim, J. K., Geiger, N., & Lengieza, M. L. (2019). Climate change marches as motivators for bystander collective action. *Frontiers in Communication, 4*, 4. https://doi.org/10.3389/fcomm.2019.00004

514. Dunlap, R. E., McCright, A. M., & Yarosh, J. H. (2016). The political divide on climate change: Partisan polarization widens in the U.S. *Environment: Science and Policy for Sustainable Development, 58*(5), 4–23. https://doi.org/10.1080/00139157.2016.1208995

515. Guber, D. L. (2013). A cooling climate for change? Party polarization and the politics of global warming. *American Behavioral Scientist, 57*(1), 93–115. https://doi.org/10.1177/0002764212463361

516. Randall, R., & Hoggett, P. (2019). Engaging with climate change: Comparing the cultures of science and activism. In P. Hoggett P. (ed.), *Climate psychology. Studies in the psychosocial* (pp. 239–261). Palgrave Macmillan, Cham.

517. Weir, K. (2018). Climate change is our call to action. *APA Monitor*, *49*(10), 42. https://www.apa.org/monitor/2018/11/cover-climate

518. Ingle, H. E. (2020). Perspectives on climate justice for psychology. *Clinical Psychology Forum*, *332*, 16–20.

519. Knight, K. (2020). Climate activism as a clinical psychologist. *Clinical Psychology Forum*, *332*, 40–44.

520. Capstick, S., Whitmarsh, L., Poortinga, W., Pidgeon, M., & Upham, P. (2015). International trends in public perceptions of climate change over the past quarter century. *Wiley Interdisciplinary Reviews: Climate Change*, *6*(1), 35–61. https://doi.org/10.1002/wcc.321

521. Corner, A., Whitmarsh, L., & Xenias, D. (2012). Uncertainty, scepticism and attitudes towards climate change: Biased assimilation and attitude polarisation. *Climatic Change, 114,* 463–478. https://doi.org/10.1007/s10584-012-0424-6

522. Hornsey, M. J., Harris, E. A., Bain, P. G., & Fielding, K. S. (2016). Meta-analyses of the determinants and outcomes of belief in climate change. *Nature Climate Change, 6,* 622–626. https://doi.org/10.1038/nclimate2943

523. McDonald, R. I., Chai, H. Y., & Newell, B. R. (2015). Personal experience and the 'psychological distance' of climate change: An integrative review. *Journal of Environmental Psychology, 44,* 109–118. https://doi.org/10.1016/j.jenvp.2015.10.003

524. Bolton, M. J., Ault, L. K., Burton, K., Allen, D. R., & Mogil, H. M. (2021). Measuring epistemic weather curiosity: Initial validation of a self-report, individual difference questionnaire. *PsyArxiv,* preprint. https://doi.org/10.31234/osf.io/pv6ar

525. Stewart, A. E. (2017, December). *Assessing weather curiosity in university students*. Presentation at the Annual Meeting of the American Geophysical Union, San Francisco, CA.

526. Bowden, K. A., Heinselman, P. L., Kingfield, D. M., & Thomas, R. P. (2015). Impacts of phased-array radar data on forecaster performance during severe hail and wind events. *Weather and Forecasting*, *30*(2), 389–404. https://doi.org/10.1175/WAF-D-14-00101.1

527. Bowden, K. A., & Heinselman, P. L. (2016). A qualitative analysis of NWS forecasters' use of phased-array radar data during severe hail and wind events. *Weather and Forecasting*, *31*(1), 43–55. https://doi.org/10.1175/WAF-D-15-0089.1

528. Clark, A. J., Jirak, I. L., Gallo, B. T., Roberts, B., Knopfmeier, K. H., Clark, R. A., Vancil, J., Dean, A. R., Hoogewind, K. A., Heinselman, P. L., Dahl, N. A., Krocak, M. J., Choate, J. J., Wilson, K. A., Skinner, P. S., Jones, T. A., Wang, Y., Creager, G. J., Reames, L. J., ... Weiss, S. J. (2020). A real-time, simulated forecasting experiment for advancing the prediction of hazardous convective weather. *Bulletin of the American Meteorological Society*, *101*(11), E2022–E2024. https://doi.org/10.1175/BAMS-D-19-0298.1

529. Wilson, K. A., Heinselman, P. L., & Kang, Z. (2016). Exploring applications of eye tracking in operational meteorology research. *Bulletin of the American Meteorological Society*, *97*(11), 2019–2025.

530. Wilson, K. A., Heinselman, P. L., Kuster, C. M., Kingfield, D. M., & Kang, Z. (2017). Forecaster performance and workload: Does radar update time matter? *Weather and Forecasting*, *32*(1), 253–274. https://doi.org/10.1175/WAF-D-16-0157.1

531. Wilson, K. A., Heinselman, P. L., & Kuster, C. M. (2017). Considerations for phased-array radar data use within the National Weather Service. *Weather and Forecasting, 32*(5), 1959–1965. https://doi.org/10.1175/WAF-D-17-0084.1

532. Wilson, K. A., Heinselman, P. L., Skinner, P. S., Choate, J. J., & Klockow-McClain, K. E. (2019). Meteorologists' interpretations of storm-scale ensemble-based forecast guidance. *Weather, Climate, and Society, 11*, 337–354. https://doi.org/10.1175/WCAS-D-18-0084.1

533. Cross, R. N., & LaDue, D. S. (2020). When uncertainty is certain: A nuanced trust between emergency managers and forecast information in the Southeast U.S. *Weather, Climate, and Society*, early online release. https://doi.org/10.1175/WCAS-D-20-0017.1

534. Ernst, S., LaDue, D., & Gerard, A. (2018). Understanding emergency manager forecast use in severe weather events. *Journal of Operational Meteorology*, *6*(9), 95–105. https://doi.org/10.15191/nwa-jom.2018.0609

535. Baumgart, L. A., Bass, E. J., Phillips, B., & Kloesel, K. (2008). Emergency management decision making during severe weather. *Weather and Forecasting*, *23*(6), 1268–1279. https://doi.org/10.1175/2008WAF2007092.1

536. Hoss, F., & Fischbeck, P. (2016). Increasing the value of uncertain weather and river forecasts for emergency managers. *Bulletin of the American Meteorological Society*, *97*(1), 85–97.

537. League, C. E., Diaz, W., Philips, B., Bass, E. J., Kloesel, K., Gruntfest, E., & Gessner, A. (2010). Emergency manager decision-making and tornado warning communication. *Meteorological Applications*, *17*(2), 163–172. https://doi.org/10.1002/met.201

538. Kox, T., Lüder, C., & Gerhold, L. (2018). Anticipation and response: Emergency services in severe weather situations in Germany. *International Journal of Disaster Risk Science, 9*, 116–128. https://doi.org/10.1007/s13753-018-0163-z

539. Xu, Z. (2020). How emergency managers engage Twitter users during disaster. *Online Information Review, 44*(4), 933–950. https://doi.org/10.1108/OIR-08-2019-0275

540. Roberts, S. S., & Wernstedt, K. (2019). Decision biases and heuristics among emergency managers: Just like the public they manage for? *The American Review of Public Administration, 49*(3), 292–308. https://doi.org/10.11770275074018799490

541. Liggett, A. J., Yalda, S., & Klockow-McClain, K. (2020). *Expert judgment versus yours: Understanding local flood risk perceptions*. Unpublished master's thesis, Millersville University. http://www.amberliggett.com/research.html

542. Cross, H. A., Cavanaugh, D., Buonanno, C., & Hyman, A. (2021). The impact of the Storm Prediction Center's convective outlooks and watches on emergency management operational planning. *Journal of Operational Meteorology*, *9*(3), 36–46. https://doi.org/10.15191/nwa-jom.2021.0903

543. Bolton, M. J., Ault, L. K., Greenberg, D. M., & Baron-Cohen, S. (2018). Exploring the human side of meteorology: A brief report on the psychology of meteorologists. *Journal of Operational Meteorology*, *6*(3), 23–32. https://doi.org/10.15191/nwajom.2018.0603

544. Bolton, M. J., & Ault, L. K. (2020). Weathering the storms: Workplace wellbeing, mental health, and the U.S. meteorologist. *International Journal of Undergraduate Research and Creative Activities*, *12*(1), 1-13. https://doi.org/10.7710/2168-0620.0293

545. Vermeulen, K. (2014). Understanding your audience: How psychologists can help emergency managers improve disaster warning compliance. *Journal of Homeland Security and Emergency Management, 11*(3), 309–315. https://doi.org/10.1515/jhsem-2014-0055

Matthew J. Bolton is a graduate student at Saint Leo University. With involvement in professional meteorology dating back to high school, he has had a life-long passion for meteorology. He has published over 30 scholarly papers, empirical and otherwise, with the psychology of weather and climate a major focus of his studies and writing. Currently a volunteer crisis counselor, Matt plans to pursue a career in mental health counseling, with one focus on natural disaster mental health. This is his first book.

Matt can be reached for comments and questions, by email at psychwxbook@gmail.com and on Twitter @matthewbolton__ (two underscores). Visit his website at www.mattbolton.me.